A JOURNEY TO PLANT SPIRIT MEDICINE

San Pedro & Ayahuasca

Humberto Fortuna MA, MS

Scoop for Seniors LLC

ISBN 9798561628092

Cover design by: Valeria Claiman

Library of Congress Control Number: 2018675309

Printed in the United States of America

I want to dedicate this book to all those individuals that are searching for that precious balance and inner peace while achieving that high frequency of satisfaction and love.

To those individuals that always support me and listen to my ideas, comments, messages and conversations...

To Source, Angels, Guides and Ancestors; the ones that gave me the courage, knowledge and guidance to create this book while they used me as a Bridge of Information and a Messenger...

To San Pedro Plant Spirit Medicine, that made me see beyond my pain, my drama and broken heart... It taught me to see myself as the beautiful creator and manifestor that I am, while accepting and recognizing my gifts and messages not just for others, but for myself as well.

To that special Shaman from Bolivia, who initiated me and taught me about diverse Energy Healing methods with unconditional love and knowledge... The one who told me once, "Do not Concentrate on the Pain...You open doors on many levels, never forget that..."

To my journey...
Thank you, thank you, thank you.

CONTENTS

PROLOGUE

I consider myself compassionate and a person of service who enjoys helping others. I realize that I have been a person of service for a very long time. From an early age, I was always able to see the needs of others and was always willing to help. Obviously, this sounds like a wonderful way to be, but when we do this without limits, or we overdo it without protecting ourselves, it is not so good.

Taking time to discover and align ourselves with Source, or whoever or whatever you believe in, is when we begin the process of discovering ourselves. It is not uncommon to begin this process when we find ourselves in difficult moments of our lives. I believe it is not relevant, when, or at what age we begin this process. The most important thing is to begin.

It is wonderful to be compassionate, but a song comes to mind by Freddy Mercury, 'Too Much Love Can Kill You.' I always get messages from song lyrics. It reminded me that too much of being of service without limits was not good for myself or others. Balancing and understanding the importance of limits, laws, and rules is important, and they need to be taken seriously. They were created for specific situations. Being able to understand them and receive their messages can help you in your process of evolution, learning, and discovery of yourself.

Being a person of service is rewarding, but preparation and limits do apply to this situation as well. Again, we talk about balance. For many years, I thought that I was on the correct path and fulfilling my mission in life by helping others. I did not take the time to protect myself while allowing situations that created emotional pain. These situations could have been preventable if I had had the correct training, information, and understanding. I should have approached these situations with feeling good, pleasure, happiness, and love.

Even though my intentions were set correctly, my knowledge and my self-care were not there yet. I was not able to protect myself because I was ignorant about many things that I should have been doing.

I was letting my obsession and my fears, along with my ego, control my emotions, while leading me to situations where I felt that I was not giving enough, and this feeling was creating a heavy weight on me. I started questioning if I had enough of other things as well, such as money, success, happiness and relationships.

Though other people saw me as a perfect, well put-together, successful entrepreneur, I was feeling the opposite. I felt that everything that I had achieved was not giving me what I was looking for. Many people did not understand me and wondered, "How could I not be happy, how could I be depressed or how could I question if I was on the right path in my life?"

The feeling was not pleasant. The idea of having achieved so many things was not giving me the happiness it should. The idea of having so many possibilities to do professional things was not a plus in my thoughts and eventually became a negative.

Of course, we all have our ups and downs. Sometimes, in our downs is when a revelation can come to us and lead us to search our souls or get in touch with our inner being.

It begins by being truthful to yourself about what you want and what you feel, what you want to do, and how you want to live your life along your current journey. Commitment is important in order to achieve the happiness and pleasure you desire.

As a middle-aged man, I thought that I had everything under control in my life, and then I realized that I was missing true happiness, balance, and peace.

I questioned myself, why? How come? The results of my soul searching were based on limits, love, and understanding that everything begins from within. Everything was about Humberto and his desire, the clear and specific desire. This process was not about forgetting the past and starting all over again. The idea was for me to respect and value what was achieved and to evolve in those areas where I was unable to achieve a balance and peaceful state of mind.

This process is very personal and is one where you cannot hold anything back. My fears, ego, and obsessions were there to challenge me all the time. Once you can identify those thoughts that lead you down the wrong path, you can become more conscious of what you want to modify on your current journey.

I believe that I always wanted to evolve, to learn, and to investigate how to improve things in business situations. Therefore I began looking for all of the resources available to me.

Having a clinical mind, and being in the Health Care industry for such a long time, where I had to challenge myself and allow my inner feelings, intuition and perception to take an important role, I had to now learn how to apply that to my personal life in areas that I was holding back or keeping hidden. I had to respect myself and find a natural manner in which to achieve that state of peace and balance that I was looking for.

The process was very interesting and revealing. It took me

getting in touch with my inner child and how I saw life then, and how I see it now. The outcome was very surprising. While being in a state of inner searching, I realized that as a child I was able to understand and interpret situations in a more holistic and natural way. This understanding is what led me to keep everything inside, and to wait to bring ideas and thoughts out due to a fear of not being understood and a fear of not being fully able to understand, at a very young age.

I knew that I was not crazy and being the analytical person that I am, I knew that I had to understand, study and emerge myself in this subject in order for me to fully understand why I felt different.

Obviously, I have been carrying these feelings ever since. As an adult, I have become more verbal and more conscious that my ideas, feelings and messages that I was receiving, needed to be taken seriously. Everything became more clear as I did my soul searching and got in touch with my inner self. It was then that I discovered the balance and peace needed to complete my journey.

Today I realize that everything is part of a timed divined plan. Now, I understand why I always felt the need to take the time to study and dedicate time to those messages, feelings and ideas that I had as a child.

And so my journey begins....

NOTES
Somehow, at this moment, my guides and angels are whispering in my ear and telling me to utilize my education and my teaching technique experience to communicate some messages to you. I realize that some chapters of this book have sections with

academic information with the purpose of generating a baseline or common ground for everyone to understand.

It is important for me to share as well that we cannot be 100% connected to Source throughout our journey or to vibrate to a high frequency without grounding ourselves at times. The idea of being connected to Source at a high level frequency would be totally unbalanced and unrealistic. Being able to sustain balance and patience all the time is the most difficult event in our journey.

Just think about how important it is to be connected with Mother Earth. Being grounded is the base of being here. It's like a tree being connected to the earth with its roots but still being able to grow while connecting to the universe.

I would like to clarify a few things about this book. This book is for every entity that resonates with love, energy healing and alternative methodologies on how to approach some issues.

I will be using the word SOURCE throughout the book as representing the Universe, God, Higher Powers or whoever you believe in that is watching and working with you.

Even though my teacher/ initiator in the energy healing world does not like to be called a Shaman, I may refer to her as a Shaman, a Healer, a Ceremony Coordinator or a facilitator. Since they are all different from each other, keep in mind that many Light Workers and Energy Healers are doing and providing Ayahuasca and San Pedro Ceremonies.

CHAPTER 1 : THE JOURNEY

"You may be feeling unrecognized, unappreciated and misunderstood. This is simply because you are ascending and your vibration is no longer a frequency match to those who have chosen not to shift at this time."   Anonymous

INTENTION

It is not the intention of this book to indoctrinate or push any specific idea or religion of any kind on anyone. This is a free will book, (at one's own discretion) and it is created with the intention of delivering a message from a person of service.

After I attended a San Pedro ceremony, I began to get messages from my angels and guides, telling me to deliver the messages that I receive. I am just sharing my experiences as a human being who is healing and evolving in an energetic and spiritual world.

In this book, I will acknowledge my current past and my past lives and I will honor and cherish my ancestors and my guides as I continue to develop my life.

A Journey to Plant Spirit Medicine is a combination of a man evolving in a spiritual world along with the clinical western medicine and sacred plants or alternative medicines. I believe that we should consider complementary and alternative medicines in a holistic manner as part of our lifestyle in these times.

I will share with my readers, the importance of understanding happiness in the work environment as part of their own personal happiness. I hope to guide or spark some light in someone's life through my experiences with my journeys to San Pedro and Ayahuasca Plant Spirit Medicine Ceremonies.

I am far from a Shaman, Curandero or any other title that you may want to give me. I want to be considered a Messenger and an Educator, and as a person of service as my guides told me to be at a San Pedro ceremony.

San Pedro, also known as Grandfather Tobacco, showed me that with self-acceptance, clear intention and desire, that everything is possible and easy to achieve in an organic manner.

As a healthcare professional for over 25 years, specializing in the geriatric field, I must confess that this journey was a total self-transformation; intellectually, academically and spiritually, to say the least. I liken it to a rebirth.

Throughout the book, you will be able to find historical and clinical information as well as energetic and spiritual information. I will talk about the benefits of the Plant Spirit Medicine and its healing properties, effects, legality and all the details related to the plant ceremony. You will be able to know the importance of preparing yourself before attending a Plant Spirit Medicine Ceremony.

You will understand how this preparedness can be applied in many other practices such as conventional treatment, where the end result will benefit you.

You will be able to understand how my clinical, traditional and academic knowledge coincides and interacts with the benefit of the San Pedro medicine as well as with Ayahuasca. I truly believe there is a bridge between traditional and alternative medicine.

It is my intention to be able to give you new ideas on how to incorporate new behaviors and new ways of thinking. My hope is that these new approaches will benefit you throughout your journey should you choose to implement them.

This book is dedicated to all those individuals who are receptive to making changes in their lives while healing past and recent issues and traumas. Hopefully, this book will give you the information that you have been searching for and the courage to confront your fears, troubles, obsessions, dramas and all of those things that hold us back or make us deviate from our path toward happiness.

FEELING NOT UNDERSTOOD?
Many times, in my professional career, I have felt misunderstood. All the dreamers, innovators, and over achievers are laughing now as they can completely relate to this comment. You may have also heard, "You're not ready yet," or "You can't do this," or "You should just give up because you're crazy."
Well, crazy we may be, but maybe not!
Maybe, we just believe in ourselves and trust our gut instincts. It is true that we do get a little crazy about an idea or thought while we are finding solutions or fulfilling a void.

After I reached my 50th birthday, I started taking the time to think seriously about what to do with my career and what direction I wanted to take personally. Many would call this a 'midlife crisis' but I knew inside me that it was much more than that.

I knew that I could do anything that I put my mind to with a clear intention, hard work and a strong desire. I knew that anything and everything was possible because I had proved it to myself over and over. I knew how to manifest a desire and achieve goals and be happy while doing it.

I knew that I had to go beyond a typical business plan and a traditional path. I was always focused on tangibles and professional goals, but there was something I owed myself for a long, long time. That missing part was beyond what I was able to achieve in a professional world.

I began a more spiritual journey while searching for that missing link. I had experienced 'The Law of Attraction' for many years, which saved my sanity, and my career, in a way, but I know now that there is so much more to discover.

In my life, I have experienced what it is to be in the dark as well as at the bottom of the bottom of depression. My friend, Cindy, who I wrote the book, "Everything You Need to Ask When Selecting an Assisted Living Facility" with, called it 'being on the edge of the edge.' Of course, that phrase became our inside joke.

I experienced firsthand what it is to be in the state of mind where nothing really matters more than your happiness; not money, acquisitions or career is important if you are not happy and balanced.

I realized that recreating myself, after being so down emotionally, was getting harder and harder as well as being very painful and requiring a tremendous amount of energy.

I started questioning myself, "Did I really know what happiness was all about?" While I was searching, I wondered how people viewed me, and which, if any of those views impacted me personally. I started getting more honest with myself and my feelings while taking responsibility for why I was feeling this way or that.

I needed to go deeper than how people's opinions of me made me feel. I had been doing that for 50 years, and I was looking to change from what I had done in the past. Once I became honest and responsible with my feelings, I began going deeper and deeper, until I realized that I needed to be in touch with my inner child and go back as far as I could recall since conception.

The process was challenging. I needed to accept what was going through my mind and assume the responsibility for my feelings. I encountered moments when I realized that I needed to resolve and work through them. I saw that many things I felt as a child were similar to what I was feeling as an adult. Those moments were ignored and not given the proper care and time needed.

I started understanding why I was able to achieve success; how it all happened, and how I did it. I started respecting my dedication and clear vision which led me to do things I believed in. I was beginning to accept and honor myself as an evolving human being in this physical body.

I realized that everything evolved to manifestation without consciously knowing the steps to get there. I did it in a very organic manner, not realizing that I was possibly recalling how to do it from past lives and with the help of my ancestors.

Every time I started a new business or project, I always concentrated on the ultimate goal and believed in that goal with passion and focus. I always did projects that I believed in and ones with a social or productive cause for society. Many of my businesses became profitable and some did not. They all have something in common; I never made money the ultimate goal. I always started a business with passion and with a mission to do the best job possible. Later, I realized that the business attracted financial gain because of its organic work and development while having a clear goal.

Throughout my life, I had never shared these personal experiences with my parents until recently; during my personal discovery journey. I knew that I was different and my feelings were misunderstood many times. When I expressed my opinions, I was criticized and hurt. On many occasions I was called or referred to as 'EL LOCO' (the Crazy One). I began my journey by not feeling understood as a child, and this continued throughout my adult life just because I saw things through a different lens. Fortunately, these situations never stopped me from fulfilling my dreams and desires.

After I figured out why I was successful, I began asking myself, "Why am I still feeling a void?" A true need to feel happy began when I started questioning about why I was not feeling joyful.

I realized through my personal discovery that there were many things that were very important to me such as honor, respect, loyalty, balance and peace. These were key in my life as well as creativity, belief, gratefulness, humility and a clear vision.

I must admit that I did not begin practicing gratefulness and humility until I understood its power and its ability to give true healing, until later in my life.

Knowing yourself and believing and trusting yourself and your intuition is the true secret. Since my childhood, I knew that I needed to believe in myself.

I knew that I was different because I had a very quick and multitasking mind. I had ideas and feelings that were defined in me from the age of 6 or 7. I knew that things had a logical side as well as a creative side, and having an analytical mind, I was able to think things through using my abilities, carefully and methodically. I analyzed things on a big scale and was then able to dream them and visualize them while projecting myself into those dreams. Sometimes I was able to day- dream them, as if they were literally happening physically. Now, with my knowledge and experience, I realize that I was 'Astro Traveling' as a kid. For me, it was natural and ok to do it. I knew my parents would not fully understand my thinking. Somehow, they grasped part of me with the limited information I was providing them. Without fully understanding, they were very supportive of me and my sister. I owe them 'big time' for their love and support.

As a child, part of my life was not always easy. Living in a country that was very limited and repressed, under a dictatorship was difficult. Our society had very little exposure to the outside world. From the time I was born in 1968, to the time democracy was achieved in 1983, living in Argentina was hard to deal with.

Argentina was going through the 'Dirty War' from 1976 to 1983. Thousands of people were killed; opponents of the government as well as innocent victims. Just imagine how difficult it was to express oneself at all during that time.

For the middle and lower classes, hard times were the norm. Traveling or buying a new car was out of the question. I remember, on Sundays, having Italian pasta with my family and dreaming about flying to China or Disneyland. We would all say, "One day we will go!" even though we felt that day would never come. These were very dark moments in my life.

On top of everything else, let's add a mother who would say, "Those things are not for us anyway. That's for people who have money, not for us." Instead of her giving us hope and dreams, she would reinforce that these things were not possible for us. My father worked two jobs all of his life, and my mother worked as a private nurse and a great administrator of our home and my father's paycheck.

The crazy thing in my family was that, even though we were told there are things we were not able to afford or have, I learned how important hard work and education were. Maybe my family had a limited vision and did not have a dreamer's mind, but they had clear objectives about work ethic and goals. They were able to achieve a lot of things in a country that was always changing and unstable. They were able to buy things on credit and pay for them in totality. After saving for a whole year, we were able to go on a vacation to a beach house they rented for a full month.

At times, even though it was difficult, my parents were able to achieve their goals and their family desires. They showed me that they had a clear intention and were able to plan and reach their goals. This was an important lesson for me.

In my preteen years, I realized I was getting more determined to achieve things with dedication, hard work, and believing in myself. Believing in myself was the only thing I had during those days in Buenos Aires. The country went from a dictatorship to democracy, and things were changing all the time. So was I. I knew that I was different sexually since I was around 5 or 6. I did not have the support or the inner strength to confront society. Argentina was a 'machista' (macho) society where even my liking or playing classical music was a way of linking me to the gay community. I did not fight it but I did not embrace it either. Those who did were either kidnapped or sent to prison.

When you see yourself in a country or in a family that was limited due to financial status or overall environment, it is hard to survive and be positive, let alone, dream. But I did it anyway. Every time my mom would say, "This is not for us, it's only for rich people," I used to say, "Why not? It will be for me one day."

I remember getting the newspaper and looking for properties for sale. I always wanted to be on my own and be independent. I also remember having a calculator and working the numbers to see how much I had to save and for how long. Already, I was visualizing it and setting a clear intention and desire. I was able to achieve it many years later and many times.

I realize now what I was doing then without knowing it consciously. I was visualizing and setting an intention so strong that I was able to focus on my true desire. Through the years, with education and hard work, I can say that I was able to fulfill that desire via manifestation in many ways. I was able to buy my own homes, help my sister buy her first and second home, give my family nice vacations to Disney Parks and take my parents to China for three weeks for their 50th anniversary. I watched them enjoy my own manifestation. In time, my manifestation benefitted the people I loved, not just myself.

After the years of searching clinically and spiritually for the reasons people did not understand me, I realized that the most important person in my life was the one who needed to understand me. That was me!

Once I understood myself, accepted and protected myself with love, everything began to make sense in a more organic and holistic manner and I was able to start a new healthier and peaceful life.

I began to understand that I AM LOVE. Everything began when I started loving myself with all my gifts and faults. Recognizing myself with my gifts was a moment of being reborn. With education and purpose, I was able to align myself mentally, spiritually and emotionally.

While in this process, the learning journey allowed me to begin confronting my fears, judgments and disappointments.

What is important and what I want to get across is that you must have a desire, a clear intention and consistency in taking responsibility for your actions, and be able to confront your fears. You have to be true to yourself, create your own society within the society that governs you. You must have a clear understanding that you come to this physical body, not to suffer or stay in pain, but to evolve, enjoy life, and to be happy.

So, while I was upset in the past that no one understood me, I realize now that everything had to begin within me, and I was the first person that had to understand me. I had to embrace myself so that I could move forward and accept all the wonderful things that life had in store for me.

OPENING YOUR MOUTH

Learning when to open our mouths and give an opinion is a process that we all must confront at some point. There are many times when we should avoid expressing our opinions in order to protect ourselves and not waste our energy. In a way, it's like not letting our egos get involved in situations just to make us feel that we should say something and be a participant in the conversation. Some people feel that they have to express their opinion all of the time, or they need to be the center of a conversation or event. I have learned to pick and choose when I give my opinion. I have also learned that sometimes people will not understand my point of view, and it would be a waste of energy to express my opinion. At times, I know, and I still do it, but if my intuition says, "don't do it," I have learned to keep quiet.

I have realized that practicing this way of communicating helps me to keep my focus on my goals and to maintain balance. It also helps me to respect myself, my energy and gifts at the same time.

When I practice this new behavior, I realize that I am honoring my feelings and valuing and appreciating myself. I use this technique to remind myself of who I am, where I am, and how I got to where I am today. However, I am what I am, and I need to respect and embrace it and be grateful at the same time. I have started concentrating and valuing the love that I have for myself and how much I care for others. We have a lot to give, a lot to learn, and a lot to offer. As a person of service, I am always learning, communicating, and healing myself and others. This type of communication is very important as we are a mirror to each other. We cannot allow the fears and insecurities of others reflect back on us.

Another issue, that I've learned how to handle, is the need to control distractions. Distractions will generate a waste of energy and feelings that will not contribute to our happiness. It can generate and create doubt and mislead us to do things that we were not planning to do. Distraction can take you out of alignment, and you will need to consciously redirect yourself to refocus and realign yourself with the project you were on.

We can say that distractions will not contribute to peace and balance in your life, nor will they contribute to knowledge, since you were not consciously waiting to be distracted. You will want to find the balance between solidarity and individuality, as they are totally different from each other. We need to understand that we are enough, and we have enough with who we are. Our goal on this journey is to continue learning and evolving at our own pace. We all evolve in our own time.

Each person has different goals and objectives to achieve. As we evolve on our journey, we begin to realize what is truly important to each of us. This is why I believe that San Pedro medicine helped me to find a higher sense of myself, while connecting me to the universe.

Because I am a professional singer, a friend asked me at a dinner party if I wanted to be a famous singer. My reply was, "I just want to be happy, at peace, and balanced." My answer was a surprise to him. My thinking was, "What is fame without happiness, peace and balance?" I have had many enjoyable moments in the spotlight, and hearing the sound of applause from performing in theaters in Buenos Aires, Argentina, to beautiful theaters in Florida. I did not know how to enjoy it to the fullest and feel that good feeling of being appreciated, due to the fact that I was not balanced and at peace at that time. I followed my answer to his question by mentioning how grateful I was for what I was able to achieve.

While I am in the process of writing this book, I am receiving messages that continually flow throughout my being. It's the desire of being connected that continues that communication with my guides and angels. I can only say that this is a confirmation for me, as a messenger and a person of service, and I cannot say enough how much I respect this feeling. As a matter of fact, this takes me back to my first San Pedro ceremony where I felt that I had to be of service to others and not myself. Even though the Shaman realized it and told me to work on myself, I was able to receive the messages for those individuals and 'hold space' for them.

Holding space means to be with someone without judgment. It's like donating your energy, ears and heart without holding anything back. It's about practicing empathy and compassion. Holding space means to put your feelings and needs aside and allow someone to 'just be.' At this first ceremony, I realized that being of service to others was a good feeling, but after the ceremony, when I was processing why I was behaving that way, I knew that I was not the person who should be 'holding space' for others at that time. The learning was beyond that. I was learning much easier steps than holding space for others, which was how to be humble and grateful, and not just a channel for others. I have learned the importance of myself for that role, as well as being protected through my learnings.

Because I was under the effect of the medicine at one point, I saw that I was concentrating and observing other people's behaviors and reactions to the medicine. I was concentrating on the pain that they were going through. The Shaman came close to me and asked me how I was doing. When I told her what I was experiencing, she said to me, "Do not concentrate on the pain..."

At that point, I realized I had to shift my thoughts and set my ego aside, while allowing the process to follow its course. The lesson for me was that I needed to concentrate on the solution and whatever was going to give me peace, balance and happiness, even if the event was terrible and painful.

While writing this section, I feel like this is the time to listen to myself and continue learning and modifying my behaviors and patterns that I have been carrying from who knows how many years or even centuries, and take the time to accept, learn, and allow the messages to be assimilated into my thoughts, life, and routine. And that is a lot!

Prioritizing and focusing on your intention and desire, while setting your ego aside, is important. Ego is not always bad. I can truly understand the importance of being in control consciously, being here in the now and reminding myself that people need to take the first step to heal themselves. I better rephrase this.

The healing process has no specific time to begin, as well as no specific time to end. I believe that we are in a constant healing process as part of our evolution. We, as individual entities, need and desire that healing. We need to be ready to take responsibility and put the energy towards our healing process, so we can start looking at possible solutions that will lead us to the correct treatments.

Again, I would like to address the importance of not just seeing ourselves from the spiritual point of view, but also from the clinical view. Obviously, the combination of traditional, organic and natural treatments is my mission on this journey. This book is honest proof that the grouping of these treatments has had a tremendous change, impact, and benefit in my life. If you are reading this book at this moment, it is because I was supposed to write this book for you to read. It is my humble and honest desire to reach those individuals who resonate with my vibration.

Part of what you learn from the Plant Spirit Medicine experience is that people need to ask for help. Healers can't do it for them. People need to walk their own journey and ask for help when they are ready. They have to take responsibility for their needs and solutions.They must go through the healing process in their own time.

It is important for me to mention that each of us has the gift of healing ourselves and others. We need to prepare ourselves to discover our gifts. On many occasions, it is a matter of remembering from past lives, as well as searching for information to prepare and protect ourselves. The San Pedro and Ayahuasca ceremonies showed me that we are all able to do these things and much more. I believe in you and your ability to do it.

Everything I am writing about comes from messages that I received during my last San Pedro ceremony. After participating in the ceremonies, I continue to process and receive messages that my mind slowly understands in a conscious manner. I usually spend the next day by myself and in silence. Everything else disturbs my thoughts, and I want to let the messages come through and learn how to interpret them consciously.

It is important for your conscious and your subconscious to meet during and after the ceremony. I try not to push myself to try to immediately understand the meaning of the messages, but to allow myself to just flow with them while receiving them, so I can learn and share with my readers. This is part of my intention and my mission.

CHAPTER 2: THE SEARCH

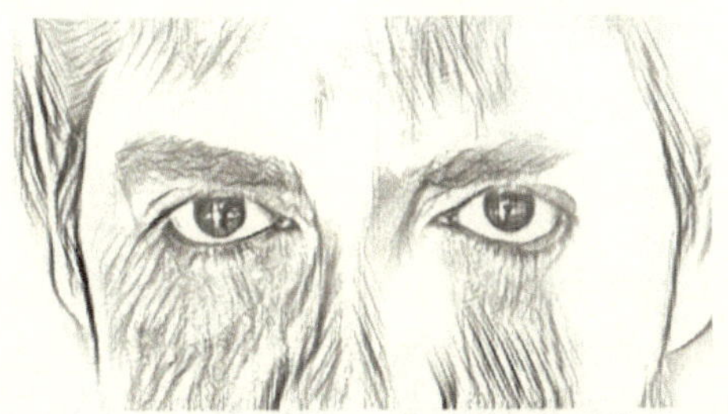

"You may feel as if you are on a battlefield, but this conflict within will come to an end as soon as you stop defending yourself. You are not here to prove yourself to others. Instead, approve of yourself. Know that your angels are on your side and that the universe is thanking you for being the authentic kind and loving soul that you are."   Alyonna Angelica

HAPPINESS AND CONTROL

Some people think that happiness is based on circumstances and situations. Most people think they would be happy if they just had more money, or if they could just find the perfect mate, or if they had better health, or if they could reach this goal or that one. Many believe that happiness is attached to a specific event or situation.

In my opinion, happiness is not attached to a specific situation but in how you approach that situation. An event can give you pleasure for a determined time frame. Most of the events that we experience are uncontrolled. They are uncontrolled by us because we have no control over how long we can sustain that good feeling that we are experiencing, since we are projecting our desires on something or someone other than ourselves. We can control and manage the attitude we have toward a situation. Think about that!

If we show our desire to the Universe, God or a Higher Power, we will be able to achieve happiness. When we put our trust in a higher power, the Universe will help us to achieve our desires. Once we put our trust in our desires and beliefs, we will attain our desires organically. There is no other way to attain manifestation. This is when the clear intention aligns with the desire and power of faith.

If we put our trust in other people to make us happy, we are going to be disappointed when it does not occur. We are not going to feel good. Once we put our trust in the Universe, nothing will destroy our happiness or move us so far away from our true desire. Because you are aligned and balanced, you will attain your true desire.

For example, if we put our happiness depends on the money we are going to earn or on a specific relationship that we are expecting, we are putting our efforts into something we cannot control. These things can change from day to day and hour to hour. This is because people and situations change because they are variables.

To be able to attain a level of happiness, we must trust ourselves and our desires. Without self-trust and a clear intention, it will be very challenging and almost impossible.

I am not saying that unexpected events will not impact our daily lives or happiness. I am sure that they will. Events will come to us, they will arise in our routines but they will not affect us personally to the point of interfering with our desires and our relationship with Source.

These alternative or unexpected events, as I call them, will not take you out of the control of your happiness. We must have a true and clear desire for our plan.

If we do this, we will not be disappointed, nor will we stop our journey to achieve our goal of happiness, since we are putting our happiness under our control and not leaving it up to others. If we believe and trust ourselves and our own true desires, we will be able to overcome any obstacle that life puts in our way.

We need to trust that things will happen in divine time. Once we understand this procedure, we will be more relaxed, focused and balanced and will be able to tackle any obstacle that may arise in our lives.

One of the things I practice on a daily basis is the five principles of Reiki....

Just for today, be grateful.
Just for today, let go of worry.
Just for today, let go of anger.
Just for today, work honestly.
Just for today, be kind.

Thoughts are powerful as well. I believe that once we are able to understand and control our thoughts and be more in the moment, we will not worry and get involved in the daily drama of our lives. We cannot worry about the things that are not in our control. Believe me, it is a waste of time and energy and it promotes uncertainties in many cases.

When we have these moments of weakness or misalignment that take us away from our balance and peace, we should focus on how grateful we are. Being grateful will give us the strength to re-align ourselves and our thoughts. Being grateful will allow you us to understand that it is more important to appreciate today than worry about the future. The future is unknown and we cannot control it. Therefore, concentrate on today! How we react in any given situation is one of the most important steps we can make while taking responsibility for our progress.

Do not worry about anything you cannot control and remember that nothing can take away your happiness. Stop carrying problems around that will only put weight on you and will not help you to reach your goals. We need to release and surrender so that we can stay aligned and understand Source. We need to use practices that will assist us, such as yoga, meditation, working with Mother Earth. These things will help you maintain alignment with Source, and with your desires and intentions. This is one of the keys to manifestation, and you can implement it in your daily routine.

Being grateful is the basis of our trust. Be thankful and trust in the divine plan. Be grateful that we can cut ties, release and surrender so better things can come.
Try to spot the problems that you are experiencing, and do not hold on to them. Release them so they don't take away your state of happiness. If you follow these steps, you will have a base that will be securing your happiness, and you will be able to control those negative thoughts that can disrupt your goals. If you do not cut those ties and problems, you will not be able to achieve true happiness and balance.

Most of the anger and anguish we may experience on a daily basis comes from negative thoughts that convert into emotions, and that is what we need to control. Once we learn that lesson, life will be much easier. Since negative thoughts are the ones leading us to unhappy places, being able to convert those negative thoughts into positive ones will help you follow your path to happiness, peace and balance. TRY IT, and you will be surprised how effective this change can be!

STUDYING
Sometimes life gives us clues, signals or even knowledge that we never asked for. For many years, I felt that I was different. I didn't have these feelings because I considered myself special, but because I believed that everyone was unique in their own

form, and for that reason, I always saw everyone as a special being. I had these feelings because I felt I was vibrating at a different level than others. I was not able to understand it at a young age, but it felt good and different. I felt that I related better to adults than children or someone of my own age. I also had many experiences to prove it to myself through premonitions, visualizations and dreams.

My inclination for music, from early childhood, was the vehicle that I chose and followed throughout my life, in order to channel my vibrations and sensitivity at all times, both spiritually and physically.

Music became my best friend in life. It lifted me up many times in my darkest moments, as well as pushed me to communicate with others as a professional speaker, a communicator, an educator and a performer. Vibrations, decibels, notes and harmonies are so intensely related to our bodies; much more than we think. I am passionate about continuing to educate myself as part of my personal and spiritual evolvement and growth. I always took the initiative, as a natural modality to learn and then share my knowledge with others. Now, with all this new information, I love to share the importance of vibrating in a healthy and harmonious way, on a daily basis, while exploring alternative methods and practices. The words, holistic and organic became a part of my being while allowing myself to flow with the art of allowing.

I have had many ups and downs, as we all have had to deal with, in my 50 years of life. Each time I was able to conquer them and move forward, but as I said before, I always felt something was missing. Once I was able to identify that missing link, I started the search for information that I needed to fill that void. Life works in very mysterious ways.

At the end of a marriage, I was able to turn a page in my life and begin questioning myself about what was happiness for Humberto, and what piece or pieces were missing from my life in order to reach a state of happiness. At this point, I realized that I needed to be more in touch with my inner self, my spirituality, my soul, the universe and my inner child.

I had to do some very deep soul searching so I chose to dedicate my time and energy in a conscious and responsible way to the study of the Law of Attraction, Energy Healing and Alternative Medicine.

It was very easy to begin the process because all the information that I was looking for was coming to me. I was surprised, in a way, how easy everything began to flow at this point in my life. Resonating with the power of the universe but not so knowledgeable in the subject, I understood that there was a reason that this information was coming to me. Messages were coming to me via the internet, emails, offers and even Shamans crossing my path. The funny thing is that everything was related to my journey and I was just not noticing them at the time. I was always putting those messages aside until I had the time to pay attention. When I realized that I had the time, then I was able to see that I was ready to receive the information. I know that I was always ready to dedicate myself to it, but I always postponed it, putting other personal goals first. I just needed to accept the responsibility to 'just do it.' While taking the responsibility, I wondered if I was postponing this area of study for any other reason, like avoiding something. Little did I know that I was going through a lot of healing situations and that I had to work very hard on myself. It was not going to be just reading and meditating sessions but a lot of personal work.

When I decided to allow myself to be part of this new journey, I began honoring my desires and the intention that I had already set up from a very young age. I always promised myself that one day, I would honor and study a side of me that was not understood by me or others. I decided that I would study possible gifts that I had that I had not developed. I felt that I had unintentionally and without knowing, set my intention when I was about 7 or 8, leading to the process of manifestation. I obviously set up a clear intention to learn about spirituality and other modalities. I understand that setting a clear intention will materialize and manifest itself when we are ready for it and the time is right. Now, I understand the divine plan and divine time. Everything will happen when it needs to happen as part of our journey and evolvement. Nothing will come to us that we cannot handle as hard as it may be to understand. This is how I knew that all of the information I was receiving via messages was for me to begin this new journey that would lead me to the Journey of San Pedro and Ayahuasca.

I decided to enroll myself in an Energy Healing Academy with a Bolivian Shaman, 'Light Worker'. I met her when she came to my Art Academy, Humfor Energy of the Arts in Fort Lauderdale, Florida. At that time, she came for psychodrama classes, and that is how I found out about her 'light work.' I connected with her from the very moment that I met her. I was very in tune with her teachings and vibrations. She was very detailed and had an academic style. As an academic student myself with two Master's Degrees and a Post Graduate Certificate, among other diplomas, I knew I needed this to be presented to me in an academic way. I needed to incorporate and assimilate this information so that it made sense to my brain, so I would then be able to implement it in my spiritual and energetic field.

I had the need to incorporate new knowledge and information into my current life. I knew this was more than the clinical studies and professional work that I had done for 25 years working with the geriatric population. I always believed in integration and not segregation. I consider myself a very open-minded person, open to new ideas, and all possibilities in general.

When I decided to begin this journey, I realized that I had

begun a new path in my life. Many signs and situations have manifested themselves to me in these past few years that have led me to make the decision to pay attention to my vibration and my calling. I have been leading my life with the ultimate desire to fill the void and find the missing link that I was looking.

SO I DID!

When I started recognizing and accepting the different feelings that I have had since I was a kid, I started dedicating my energy and soul to my true path. My journey began by studying alternative healing methods and practices. As a musician, I knew that music would have an important role in my development. I began understanding and implementing music and sound as a healing technique and showing how it affects the human body. I always used music with my Alzheimer's and related Dementia clients throughout my career, and I was able to see how effective it was with them by reducing their anxiety behaviors.

I became a Certified Sound Healer Practitioner, knowing that needed to be part of my evolution for the rest of my life.

I knew that I wanted to become a bridge between the old Humberto and the new Humberto that I was becoming. I wanted to bridge the clinical mind to the energetic and spiritual field. Through all of these new feelings and personal adventures, I became certified as an Energy Healer Practitioner. While practicing various types of techniques, both traditional and alternative, I found I was able to assist others on their journey to happiness.

As a Geriatric Specialist on Aging Studies and a Health Care Administrator and Consultant for over 25 years, as well as a musician and performer, I am fusing my knowledge and experience with all of these new techniques and philosophies. Being certified as a Reiki Master, Angel Therapist Practitioner, Past Lives Regression and Akashic Records Reader, I was able to integrate these modalities with my clinical and traditional background.

I am blessed, humbled and very pleased that I made this decision and have chosen to listen to my own gifts. This new path allows me to bring peace, knowledge and guidance, while providing individuals help through a more holistic and organic healing experience.

This was just the beginning of my journey.

INNER SEARCH

This is not an easy task for your ego. When you begin the search to find yourself, it will take a lot of determination, responsibility, and a clear intention for why you are doing this and what it is that you want to achieve. All of these qualities are going to become your support and a way to keep focus on your search.

For me, it was the right time, the right moment in my life. I decided to fulfill the void that I had been carrying with me since childhood. I was determined to start feeling more in balance and at peace with my career, lifestyle, body, and spirit. In a way, my intention was to become more holistically understood by myself. I was intent on discovering what true happiness was for me. I started this journey, as I said before, after a divorce, when I realized there was more than just being married and being accepted in the eyes of society.

I knew that there was much more to discover about myself and the universe. I felt it and consciously wanted to unravel the mysteries of life. I always knew that this was coming. I began to pay attention and respect my intuition. Messages were all around me, but I did not realize that those messages had been part of my life all along. I was just not paying attention to them. My inner search began with a simple question: "What was happiness for Humberto?" This was my ultimate goal or purpose in life, being able to achieve happiness on a higher level or as I like to call it, 'conscious happiness.'

After reviewing chapters of my personal life history, I began an inner search. It was like peeling the layers of an onion and putting those layers on a table to see what was missing. I realized that something essential was not there. I needed more than money, materialistic items, or people to make me happy.

I realized I needed to be in touch with my inner self, while honoring and supporting the organic Humberto. Spirituality was nowhere to be found in any of those onion layers. This was easy to understand, but hard to consciously accept. I felt empty and embarrassed for some reason. I didn't beat myself up, but I realized that now was the time to begin what I had been putting off since I was a child. I was not sure if I was doing this in the correct way, but I welcomed every step with no resistance in any way.

I was raised in a traditional Catholic family. I took my first communion, but I was never confirmed. In the course of my life, I was exposed to spiritual work. My father showed me diverse, holistic philosophies. He is a very special man, and he was always involved in physical expression art and yoga. At 83, he continues his involvement with alternative medicines and spiritual, holistic practices. He never pushed his beliefs on anyone in the family. He always told my sister and me, that if we ever wanted to learn more about the 'Escuelita Spritual work,' or research other religions and philosophies, we should do it when we became adults. He told us to study it and make sure it was a good fit for us. All this explanation came about when I asked my father why he was not taking us with him to his spiritual practices. From my father, I learned to respect and value all religions and practices.

I found music as my religion. Music was my way of communicating with the universe and God. I didn't realize that I was unconsciously synchronizing myself to the universe via music, lyrics and chords. If I think about it now, I was constantly elevating myself through music and bringing myself closer to God, as if I were going to church every Sunday, the way most people did in my town. I knew, in a way, that I was connected and would one day dedicate my energy to discovering my spirituality.

Since the age of 8, being connected to music made me feel connected to God, energy, and the Universe. I also had a special connection to Abraham and the Jewish faith for no particular reason. My love of music led me to dedicate many hours to studying, culminating in a Masters Degree and becoming a Music Professor Major in piano and chorus conducting at age 19 in Buenos Aires, Argentina.

I was unknowingly gaining spiritual knowledge through music which made me realize that I needed to concentrate more on the academic side. I can truly say today that I have never felt spiritually empty, but I have always wondered if the reason I was not spiritual was because I was not following the traditional path of the Catholic Church.

When it came to me, it presented itself so organically, just a post on Facebook. It was about a course on Energy Healing. I knew that I was ready for it. I found the right path, and I had the time. Everything was aligned and ready for me. I remember how happy I was to find that missing link. I felt full of joy and peace. I remember saying "thank you, thank you, thank you."

The inner search process became clear to me. I was feeling peace and balance, and this time it wasn't through my music, but through the journey that I was about to begin. Feeling so aligned with what I was beginning, I continued to dig deeper into my search. I had to determine what peace and balance was for me. This process took me a couple of weeks as I began questioning and thinking to try to understand what happiness was for Humberto.

I realized that all the other endeavors that I was able to achieve were not 100% in line with what I was searching for. I won't say that they are not important nor that I am not grateful for the material success they have brought me. What I realized was that the missing link was more important, more relevant to my life and to my happiness. So, I began studying with a Shaman, a teacher, a light worker in her academy.

The interesting point in my life was how everything was unfolding in perfect time. It was the right time for me to do it. It felt good. I had been waiting for this moment to dedicate the time and energy to discovering my spirituality and improving my knowledge of such.

Everything was aligned, as I said before, and I was ready for this new experience. In a way, I felt that God was holding my hands and letting me feel His love. I feel like His plan for me was to experience everything in a natural and organic way. It's like He said to me, "You will be prepared, holistically and organically and you will learn as your journey unfolds because you are wise. You will use your gifts and will enjoy them and they will support you during your ups and downs. Everything comes in a divine plan. You will experience it first in your flesh and your emotions, and one day, you will read it and you will be able to appreciate your gifts and successes". And so it was…

While writing this book, there were many times when I did things correctly without knowing why I was doing it that way. I realize now that I was guided somehow to overcome barriers and dark moments, as I followed the correct steps. I'd also like to say that it was very emotional to have my friend of 15 years say to me, "Wow, you have been doing all these things before you started this new focus in your life. I can see it and I am a part of it so just keep going."

We need to understand that being ready for anything that we are going to approach is one of the most important factors. Being ready consciously for any type of success or manifestation is a must. Otherwise, we would not be able to connect with our God or the universe. Obviously, I did not have this information when I began the process, and I didn't understand it from the rational, academic, cognitive side. I can assure you though, that I was ready to do whatever I had to do. I learned this way of thinking from seeing the success I had through hard work after coming to the US when I was 21 with $150 in my pocket 31 years ago.

Being ready is the only way that a process or learning experience will work. If you are not completely ready, you will not be able to fully benefit or understand the message, and you will never get the result you seek.

I believe that, without knowing, I was practicing the 'art of allowing.' The art of allowing me to prepare myself for that specific, divine time and be ready to learn from the academic point of view. The good thing is I never resisted learning or receiving messages from the spiritual side of me. I surrendered to whatever was part of my divine plan. I never questioned or challenged it, so I guess the universe knew that I was ready to handle whatever was presented to me. Everything aligned itself and came to me at the right moment. It was not hard for me to initiate this new path. I was ready. Being ready with a clear intention and desire is what led me to write this book as part of my learning.

CHAPTER 3: EARTH MEDICINE

Concentrate on what makes you happy and makes
you feel good, peaceful, complete and aligned because
that is the beginning of the new YOU... HF

DISCOVERING EARTH MEDICINE

When I began to walk my new path to energy healing and other alternative medicine practices, my personal and spiritual world expanded to levels I never thought I had in me. I am sure that you have experienced something similar, by reading about or witnessing energy healing, and you resonated with it.

I am a firm believer that Source sends us what we want when we do it correctly, and Source receives it with our conscious vibration. Somehow, the name of this book or the subject matter resonated or vibrated with you and that is why you are aligning with this information and with me.

It is a beautiful and marvelous experience that we encounter when we surrender to our calling, our desires and our intuition.

We all know about the importance of trees and plants in our environment and their contribution to humanity and our planet earth. The benefits from plants are invaluable and we can truly say that plants are not just for decorating our gardens or feeding our families.

When we begin researching and learning about the benefits of plants and herbs, we can understand that they heal wounds, cure headaches and ease digestion along with countless other ailments. The amazing thing is that you can get these things right in your own backyard. Isn't that wonderful? This reminds me of my ancestors and grandparents from Argentina with their Italian and Indigenous roots.

Many teas, tinctures and oils from medicinal plants were offered to me throughout my life and were consumed in my family as a natural alternative to western medicine. Instead of a pharmacy, we went to the garden.

I'm sure that many of you may have a few of these memories yourself or are today, growing herbs and plants in your own backyard to use as remedies and for cooking.

The reason that it's called Plant Spirit Medicine is for the simple reason that these medicines are generally made of plant based ingredients such as Peyote (cactus), San Pedro (cactus), Ayahuasca (vine), Psilocybin (mushrooms), Iboga (shrub).

For some of us, it is a family tradition to have a few medicinal plants to help keep us well in our backyard.

I will take the liberty to express my opinion and say this, the better known of these plant medicines is Ayahuasca, a vine-based brew made throughout South America. It seems, lately that San Pedro medicine is gaining popularity worldwide, as well.

Ayahuasca's popularity is not only being promoted by religious groups, but also by constant research, and by Western Medicine, about the benefits of the vine.

As we can see, both Alternative and Western Medicines are trying to support and learn from each other for the benefit of our well-being.

EATH vs. WESTERN TRADITIONAL MEDICINE

In past decades, we have seen more and more people become consciously aware of natural and holistic approaches to health, medicine and the food they eat. Granted, it could have been a clever marketing strategy for many companies, but for whatever reason, it has had a positive outcome and benefits.

Western medicine started with the Greek physician, Hippocrates of Cos (460-ca. 377) He is considered the father of medicine in the western world. Western Medicine is based on a system in which medical doctors and other healthcare professionals treat symptoms and diseases using traditional elements and treatments such as drugs, radiation and surgery. These healthcare professionals use allopathic medicine, biomedicine, conventional medicine, mainstream medicine and orthodox medicine.

So, why do we call it 'modern medicine?' Guess what? Modern medicine is synonymous with Western Medicine even though this medicine has its origins in the east. It is referred to as 'Western Medicine' because modern science is rooted in the philosophy of European Enlightenment. Similarly, Holistic Medicine is often synonymous with Traditional Chinese or Oriental Medicine.

Let's understand the difference between traditional and modern medicine. When we refer to traditional medicine, we need to understand how everything evolved. Traditional practitioners have historically shared their knowledge and experiences freely. They used 'open-access' before the term even existed.

As part of the evolution of medicine, we also have the evolution of laws and regulations. Modern medicine has very strict intellectual and property laws and a highly evolved patenting system used to protect knowledge about drugs and medical techniques.

Talking about Earth Medicine is talking about the healing art of working with plants, minerals and animal qualities to bring about holistic wellness in mind and spirit. When we do it consciously, the medicine seems to be potent and will flow through our body with great results.

The integral concept of why Earth Medicine is called 'medicine' is because it is used to heal our bodies and minds, while aspiring to use it to heal the planet.

Earth Medicine takes into consideration, many ancestral and traditional cultures holistically.. This type of healing, practiced by some cultures, as well as individuals, is as necessary to us as air and water. The more you practice this process, the more effective and natural healing you will experience.

This is a fantastic tool to help us understand and work with our planet and its resources, as a fantastic tool created by humankind. Earth medicine is trying to provide us with the resources needed as part of a science, so, we should respect this medicine and treat it responsibly.

PLANT MEDICINE AND SPIRITUALITY

When we start talking about plants and their medicinal powers, we can enter into a very long and interesting conversation. I will try to limit myself and only mention a few characteristics of these 'medicine plants.' I will also address how these medicine-based plants are being utilized by many cultures and have been for many years.

As part of my research and understanding, I have learned that what we call plant medicine, some people call Plant Spirit Medicine. The reason they call it this is that they recognize the plant as having an actual spirit. Plant Spirit Medicine can heal the deepest reaches of the heart and soul when it is taken, while allowing the spirit of the medicine to guide us and heal us from an ailment.

Since the beginning of time, when the traditional Shaman healer turned to the plant world, he turned to the spirit of the plants. This is why it is important to know things by appropriate name. Plant Spirit Medicine does not really mean that it will work with your spirit. What it means is that through the spirit of the plant, a healing process will be provided to whoever takes it. It is the spirit of the plant that healed the Shaman's patients. The spirits were his friends, his teachers and his allies.

Once you begin learning and preparing yourself for the medicine, you will begin connecting with the spirit of the medicine. I will talk later about the importance of finding a way to commit yourself to the medicine from the moment you make the decision to attend and throughout the ceremony.

This ancient practice, long forgotten in the west, has now been revitalized and reintroduced by healers today. Many Shamans or Healers have proven their effectiveness in today's world as in times past. Plant Spirit Medicine healers call upon the extraordinary healing powers of the plant spirits more and more these days. We see many ceremonies offering this healing today.

I would like to make it clear that plant medicine is not for recreational purposes and should be treated with respect, like any other medicine. I believe when you take any medicine into your body, you should consult the physician or the professional who is giving you that medicine. You should also research his or her experience and background.

Before you prepare yourself for a ceremony, you should take the time to make sure that you are putting your health in the hands of a reputable and professional person.

It is also important to understand the difference between Plant Spirit Medicine and other forms of herbal medicines. They differ in the importance they place on the relationship between the healer, the plants and the client.

Also, Herbalists treat a variety of physical conditions, illnesses and allergies through the holistic use of plants in conjunction with medical knowledge. Herbalists treat patients using plant based remedies as well as other treatments. Many of these complementary and alternative medicines can truly help a person holistically and organically.

Plant Spirit Medicine healers look at the person as a whole. They view the person, while leaving judgment and criticism behind. They concentrate on seeing you with all they have to offer, while believing and working with the spirit of the plant to help you.

As an Energy Healer, I can only see the person as a whole to really come to the root of the person's imbalance. Once I see the person as a whole, I can select the use of the appropriate treatment and provide them with what they need for health in their body, mind and spirit. The result is deeply effective as an organic form of healing on all levels.

I can personally say that when I take the San Pedro or the Ayahuasca Plant Spirit Medicines, I am able to work on specific problems that may not always be pleasant. The benefit of achieving clarity and healing with my issues is what made me able to concentrate and write this book. Plant Spirit Medicines allowed me to return to the feeling of balance and harmony, and to be the best version of myself.

If you believe in the medicine and you consciously surrender to its spirits, you will experience the most important and interesting discovery about yourself, while healing and evolving at the same time. It is a feeling that you will never forget.

We need to remember that our ancestors lived this way, beautifully and gracefully. They were able to live an existence where there was no separation from nature. They honored their roots, traditions and culture while protecting themselves with these Plant Spirit Medicines. Ultimately, I can say that Plant Spirit Medicine can restore us to a state of grace through its healings and teachings.

SAN PEDRO VS. AYAHUASCA

When we talk about plant medicine, the two most popular plant medicine ceremonies come to mind; Ayahuasca and San Pedro. I am not an expert on this, but I would like to share the knowledge and information that I was able to gather for you. These two Plant Spirit Medicines will be the concentration of this book and the ceremonies that have been performed by many cultures for many years.

For me, it is important to learn about many things in general, but I am never satisfied with just one sentence or comment as an explanation. I need to go to the root of the subject to fulfill my desire for knowledge. I am not saying that everyone has to do it this way, but it is my way of learning.

Let's begin by understanding the difference between San Pedro and Ayahuasca. In comparing the two, I would say that Ayahuasca is for exploration of self and the world (seen and unseen) outside of yourself. San Pedro is all about coming home to yourself.

It's difficult to describe what happens in an Ayahuasca ceremony or even in a San Pedro ceremony since each one is different, and we all have different experiences.
The purpose of preparing and drinking Ayahuasca was for spiritual and religious use by the Ancient Amazonian tribes. These days, it is being used as a sacred tea by many religious communities in North America, Central America, and Brazil. Western Medicine has been paying attention to Ayahuasca tea as potential help for people who suffer from depression and anxiety. Much research has been done, and more information on this subject can be found in the following chapters.

On the other hand, the San Pedro Plant Medicine, as it is called in many places, is a cactus brew. The Shaman or coordinator will brew the cactus for more than eight hours as part of a ritual.

This brew has a male energy and that is why many Shamans or Curanderos call it the grandfather brew as it is gentler and more delicate. There is also a San Pedro powder from the same cactus that is used as well.

San Pedro medicine is very powerful! The medicine connects you with the energy of the sun, and because of this, the ceremony has to be done outside near nature or a sacred place. It will take us to different states of consciousness where we can achieve a dissolution of unconscious complexes rooted in personal problems.

I cannot begin to tell you how important the role of the Shaman or coordinator is to the ceremony. They will be conducting the ceremony and supervising your medicine. They will be the primary pillar to guide you through this journey while working with your intentions and the Plant Spirit Medicine.

Many rituals will be performed, such as Limpias, cleansing, and healing songs that will allow you to expand your senses in order to feel grounded and let you experience the beauty of love.

The medicine will show you that you are an important part of this sacred planet and how you need to protect it, so it may continue to benefit you with its secret medicines.

Part of the teaching will help you understand why you make wrong choices and decisions and help you to resolve those issues, if that is your intention. If your desire is to have a better idea of your future, you will work more with your senses and emotions. In my last ceremony, I needed to heal my wounded heart, and the sacred plant helped me in a very kind and soft way, by showing me what I was doing wrong, as well as things I needed to work on.

The process of San Pedro can take from 12 to 15 hours. Ayahuasca ceremonies can take from 6 to 7 hours.

I would like to reiterate that you are completely conscious during these ceremonies. It works better when you are in meditation and silence, as it allows you to work and concentrate on the things that you want to work on.

WHAT CAN GO WRONG?
As much as we prepare, research and study the medicine, there can always be side effects and a few things to take into consideration. This is not to scare anyone or promote fear about plant medicine treatments. Very few people have ever had a bad

experience. Someone once said that people who have had an unpleasant experience just had a 'bad trip' or 'went to the dark side' of San Pedro.

Personally, I have never experienced a bad event in any of the ceremonies I have attended, nor have I ever witnessed one. But I would like to address the 'bad trips' as well as abuse within healing communities.

Most people have positive and transformative experiences with the implementation of San Pedro and/or Ayahuasca medicine. Unfortunately, it is not always the case, since there have been negative ones as well. These cases can leave a person with long term suffering, full-on psychosis, and suicidal thoughts. Therefore, it is very important for people who are thinking about participating in plant medicine to take precautions.

Let's begin with making sure that you have no medical conditions that would prevent you from taking psychedelics. If you have any doubt, please consult with a physician to see if the medicine is safe for you to work with. Please do not ignore your health.

As I have mentioned before, make sure that you go into a Plant Spirit Medicine ceremony with the right mindset in a safe environment. Take the time to prepare yourself. Do your homework and preparation consciously. You will have the opportunity to review everything before you go into the ceremony.

Be sure not to force any emotional content, like past trauma, that you are not ready to deal with. You know what you can handle and what you cannot. The importance of the communication with the Coordinator is crucial, and I hope you take it seriously.

When we believe in spiritual healers and Shamans, we should

also be aware that a mistake or flaw can occur in their practice as well as any other professional practice. As a healthcare provider who is currently practicing Complementary and Alternative Medicine, I can say that in this industry, like any other industry, you will find deception. There are people who use the term, 'spiritual healer' or 'alternative healer,' but they are fake or even worse, promoters of some serious dysfunction. You may encounter individuals who lack standards, have dodgy practices, and predatory relationships or more. Crime and even spiritual warfare are known to occur within such communities.

DRUG TEST
The main component of Ayahuasca, DMT (N, N-Dimethyltryptamine), metabolizes very rapidly and is undetectable in blood a few hours after ingestion and is undetectable in urine within 24 hours.

Several factors are involved in determining how long mescaline, the main component in San Pedro Spirit Medicine, is detectable in the body. The timetable for detecting mescaline in the system is also dependent upon each individual's metabolism, body mass, age, hydration level, physical activity, health conditions and other factors, making it impossible to determine an exact window for when mescaline will show up on a drug test.

Are Ayahuasca and San Pedro Medicines addictive?

There is no scientific evidence that indicates that DMT is addictive. Some reports say that some users have the desire to recreate the positive experience they had in the ceremony. This is why it is being evaluated and contemplated by traditional medicine as a therapeutic option for substance abuse disorder. I'll say again that Ayahuasca is not a drug that should be used recreationally.

San Pedro Medicine, mescaline is neither safe nor legal. Even though the drug may not be addictive, long-term mescaline and peyote abuse may overtake a person's life and cause them to experiment with other drugs which carry greater risks for addiction and overdose.

DRUG TESTING (DMT and Mescaline)

Because DMT is metabolized by the body very quickly, it is difficult to find it in the results of drug testing. The typical blood or urine analysis that is run on most common hallucinogens generally only finds trace amounts shortly after use.
It is not part of the standard drug test used for law enforcement, employment or treatment purposes. DMT might be detected if a specific test is used, and it can be detected in the lab in urine and hair follicles.

Mescaline can be detected for a shorter time with some tests, but can be visible for up to three months in other tests. The following are estimated time-frames during which mescaline can be detected by various testing methods:

- Urine: Mescaline can be detected in the urine for 2-3 days
- Blood: Mescaline can be detected in the blood for up to 24 hours
- Saliva: Mescaline can be detected in saliva for 1-10 days
- Hair: Mescaline can be detected with a hair follicle drug test for up to 90 days

On a personal note:

In today's world; and it is my belief, that Complementary and Alternative Medicine is important and should be taken seriously. I have been part of the traditional and Western Medicine world, specializing in Geriatrics for years. I have worked with many clients with Alzheimer's and related dementias, and I have seen how important traditional medicines are, while at the same time, believing Alternative Medicines may work just as well, in many cases.

The integration of both medicines would be relevant in all cases. The belief in both and their complementation is so powerful and beautiful. Working with both was my intention, and why I got my Energy Healing Certification and Practice. And, I love it!

Having the pleasure to experience Alternative and Plant Medicine as part of my journey is a blessing in itself. I have always been waiting for more and more new ways of healing and new treatments.

Even though I was exposed to Oriental and Homeopathic Medicine by my parents, I always believed that Traditional and Alternative Medicine could work together. I would like to share with you what I believe, and how they complement each other. It is important to first understand certain terminology.

Since I knew the possible effects of the Plant Spirit Medicine before attending the ceremony, I was not surprised or afraid of what I was experiencing and was able to surrender to the treatment with no resistance while allowing the medicine to work.

As a Certified Energy and Sound Healer, I began providing services at my office with Sobeyda (SoBe) Cantillano, a Registered Nurse and Healthcare Consultant, as well as a Certified Energy Healer. Together, we created Complementary and 'Alternative Medicine with a Clinical Mind' in 2019. Our energy healing treatments combine the Western Medicine approach with the Alternative Medicine approach.

We believe that everything begins from within, which includes our physical body, organs, breathing and mind. It is our position to view each individual from a holistic approach; mentally, spiritually, emotionally, physically and energetically. When we refer to 'within' we also include thoughts, consciousness, sub-consciousness and senses.

We believe in an organic approach and always see our clients from a holistic point of view. We see ourselves and our clients as part of Source and we know we come from Source; therefore, we are all connected.

The type of approach that we use on our clients, we use on ourselves as well. Seeing ourselves holistically, as a whole, is the beginning of preparing ourselves for the Plant Spirit Medicine ceremony.

CHAPTER 4: SAN PEDRO

Leave the past in the past…. But it does not mean that
the situation will never return…. Remember, you can
redirect your energy from those feelings of the past
and put your full energy on your present…HF

HISTORY & US LAW

  Based on my investigation, San Pedro medicine is used for land-
scaping purposes only in the United States. It is a psychotropic
plant whose primary substance is mescaline. It is legal only
for gardening, and its active constituents are illegal and pen-
alized. Mescaline, in all of its forms, is a controlled substance.
The use of San Pedro cactus in ceremonies has been around for
3500 years by indigenous groups in Peru. The earliest known
use comes from a stone carving that dates back to around 1300
BC. It very clearly depicts a Huachuma Shaman holding a tall
San Pedro cactus. The carving was found at the Jaguar Temple at
Chavin de Huantar in Northern Peru. This carving comes from
the Chavin culture.

Another notable discovery made at the Chavin site by Peruvian archeologist, Rosa Fung, was cigar butts made from the San Pedro cactus. This sacred cactus is seen later as a decorative motif on Peruvian ceramics like the Salinar style of 400-200BC and the Nasca urns, circa 100BC-700AD.

We need to understand that the substance from the cactus, mescaline, is a hallucinogenic drug that occurs naturally in certain cactus plants native to the South West United States, Mexico and South America. These plants include: Peyote cactus (Lophophora williamsii), San Pedro cactus (Trichocereus pachanoi) and Peruvian Torch cactus (Trichocereus peruvianus).

The use of mescaline products is illegal in the United States, as I mentioned before but peyote is recognized as a sacrament in the North American Church. It is important to mention that it has been used by Native Americans for thousands of years in religious ceremonies and for treatment of various physical ailments.

Under the 1994 American Indian Religious Freedom Act, (AIRFA), if it is used in religious ceremonies, it is exempt from its classification as a controlled drug by the FDA because mescaline is as a hallucinogen.

Mescaline is also sometimes known as:
- Peyote
- Buttons
- Moon
- Cactus

Like any other medicine, San Pedro has its side effects, as well. People who take mescaline may experience unpleasant side effects including anxiety, rapid heartbeat, tremors, hallucinations and psychosis, to name a few.

When this medicine is used in a San Pedro ceremony, the medicine may be useful for overcoming addiction, and dealing with chronic pain by relieving and recalling repressed memories in a psychotherapeutic way. San Pedro cactus, in ceremonies, will help us to heal, to grow, to learn and awaken. It assists us in reaching higher states of consciousness.

The medicine is not used for recreational purposes and should always be given under the supervision of an experienced and professional Shaman or coordinator. This is a medicine that can lead you to many answers in a higher consciousness. An experienced leader, coordinator, or Shaman will guide you through the medicine and the ceremony, while working the areas that you need to focus on, or the intention that you already prepared in advance.

After experiencing the medicine twice with a Shaman during a ceremony, I can not say strongly enough, that you need to prepare mentally, spiritually, literally and physically before you enter into this journey. The preparation is as important as the ceremony. During the preparation, you will be able to begin to understand your body, mind and soul. You will begin preparing yourself for a healing process with results, and you will be able to receive whatever the medicine has for you.

I experienced the importance of having a defined and narrow intention for the ceremony first hand. By having this information beforehand, the ceremony allows you to work on your intention organically. As I said before, the medicine takes you to a higher level of consciousness with little effort. You will never become unconscious. You will always be awake and working, and the medicine will take you where it thinks you need to work, based on your intention. The medicine will make you work on an emotional, physical, spiritual and psychic level. This is why, having a Shaman, or someone in the role of coordinator, is so important.

The use of the medicine is to assist you to realize that there is no separation between you, me, the earth and the sky. We are all one. We are all part of Source.

Once you have experienced the medicine of San Pedro, you will understand that one of its teachings is to see the importance of living in balance and harmony. The medicine is the best teacher because it teaches us to practice compassion and understanding. It will also show us how to love, respect and honor all things. It is a very special moment when you can really communicate with a tree, a plant and Source naturally and freely, while finding answers, messages and solutions to your questions and investigations.

Part of the ceremony will show you that we are all children of light. You will be able to work on your inner child as a precious and special individual human being, and you will be able to see that light within you.

We are all different and each person's experiences will be different. We are all unique beautiful souls and we are all always healing ourselves.

Understand that when you drink San Pedro, it will be a personal journey of discovery of yourself and the universe.

San Pedro helped me to understand many things and rediscover myself, so I could continue evolving in my journey happily and more balanced.

San Pedro is an experience you will never forget, and it can change your life forever. You will recall San Pedro as a day full of light and love.

The beauty of this medicine is that it lasts for 12 to 15 hours as part of the ceremony. After this period of time, an assimilation and integration period begins, reflecting on the experiences and messages you may have received during the ceremony. The treatment of this medicine continues for days, weeks and even months while you are incorporating everything consciously. Then, you begin working on the problems effectively.

Being prepared will allow you to go to a ceremony in a more relaxed and comfortable state of mind. Our minds play games when we are afraid. Wondering and worrying what is going to happen in your first ceremony will not allow you to benefit to the fullest, so, do your work before you go.

MESCALINE SIDE EFFECTS

The reason I want to explain the side effects of the medicine is because KNOWING IS POWER! Knowing will help you prepare yourself before attending the San Pedro ceremony. In my opinion, knowledge is crucial before any treatment. If you are alert and oriented, and you are choosing to participate in a San Pedro ceremony, I suggest you know all of the pros and cons. Nothing bad will happen but knowing the details, will assure you that nothing will surprise you in the middle of the ceremony. Knowing what to expect consciously will help you to stay in balance should anything unexpectedly appear during the ceremony. It is important to trust the person who will be guiding you.

It is also important to understand that knowing what you could experience can assist you or open yourself up more, so that you can benefit from the medicine in a relaxed and organic manner. I think this is the best way to take advantage of the medicine and its treatment.

These are some reported side effects of taking mescaline:

Agitation: An emotional state of nervousness or nervous excitement. When taking this medicine, this can occur out of nowhere.

Hallucinations: You may see or hear things that are not there, or have no basis in reality. This is an expected side effect when taking this medicine. Sometimes, if you do not understand what you are seeing, this can be frightening. It can cause a lot of confusion or distress.

Tachycardia: Tachycardia is a rapid heart rate of over 100 beats a minute. You need to be aware that a rapid heart rate can cause anxiety which can further speed up the heart rate.

 While these more serious effects are not common, it is important for users to be aware that taking this substance does carry risks.
    Less known common effects are seizures, loss of consciousness, and vomiting.

Other possible signs that someone might be using mescaline include:
- Changes in mood
- Difficulty sleeping
- Flushed skin
- Hallucinations
- Headaches
- Increased energy levels
- Lack of appetite
- Nausea or vomiting
- Poor coordination

LEVELS OF THE MIND
    As part of understanding how San Pedro medicine works and how we can benefit from it to the fullest, it is important to understand about Mind and Consciousness. This may be a bit clinical and academic, but it will be great information for you and will help you understand what happens during the ceremony, as well as in your mind.

As a Professional Healthcare Provider, my rational mind works from a clinical angle when I work with energy healing therapies or alternative medicines. As a Geriatric Specialist I can understand human behavior very well, and I knew, that at the San Pedro ceremony, my behavior and my state of consciousness were altered as part of the effect of the medicine.

Before I attend a ceremony, I prepare my mind, body, and spirit for weeks. Ten days prior to the ceremony is sufficient but in actuality, I had been preparing since the moment I decided to participate in a ceremony. I do that because I choose to do it. You should consider each preparation as a ritual, as I do. I begin consciously doing these rituals while honoring the medicine and myself.

Preparing a questionnaire with objectives and intentions that you would like to work on during the ceremony will be of great help to the Shaman or Coordinator. While you are doing this project, you will be able to do some soul searching, and you may identify some trauma that you may have been carrying around for some time. As part of this holistic approach, it is important to understand these steps consciously, so when they play a part in the healing process, you have a better chance of understanding the messages you will receive at the ceremony.

The importance of this process was crucial for me. This way, I was able to place everything in perspective, in order for my brain to be able to process all the information gathered. This information assisted me when I was under the influence of the medicine. It helped me to work on my problems; which was my intention.

To begin to understand what is going on in my mind during a San Pedro ceremony, we'd have to talk about 'what is mind' and 'what is consciousness.'

As part of my studies on aging, I have been working, studying and learning to understand the brain, the mind, cognitive brain diagnoses and illnesses related to the brain.

The American Heritage Dictionary of English Language defines

'mind,' thusly:
'The collective conscious and unconscious processes in a sentient organ that direct and influence mental and physical behavior'

The definition attributes mind to sentient organisms and identifies it with processes that control behavior. On the other hand, the word, 'consciousness' refers to one's awareness of thoughts, memories, feelings, sensations and environment.

It is not my intention to create a confusing and complicated chapter, but I will try to make it as simple as possible.

Let's say that both the mind and consciousness are abstractions. What this really means is that they are not concrete. On the other hand, the brain is related to both of them, but in this case, is concrete.

The mind is the process that reasons, thinks and feels. It is also the totality of consciousness and unconscious mental processes and activities.

The mind has 3 levels: the conscious, the subconscious and the unconscious. This information was very important to me because once I was able to experiment with them consciously, I was able to understand how my subconscious worked with my conscious as a team, at the ceremony.

Your conscious mind is your thinking mind. It has no memory, and it can only hold one thought at a time. It is aware of one's own existence, sensations and thoughts.

The subconscious mind stores and retrieves data. It is a databank for everything that is not in your conscious mind. The function of your subconscious mind is to store and retrieve data such as beliefs, previous experiences, memories, and your skills, etc. Your conscious mind commands, and your subconscious mind obeys. Your conscious mind works day and night to make your behavior work with your emotions and thoughts, as well as your desires.

Unconsciousness can be caused by nearly any major illness, injury, or substance abuse (drug or alcohol). For example: If you choke on something, it can lead you to become unconscious. The unconscious mind is a reservoir of feelings and thoughts that are outside of our conscious awareness. Just think of it as the data in the subconscious that creates how we interpret an experience, and whether it is positive or negative.

SAN PEDRO CEREMONY AND RULES
This beautiful process; the San Pedro Ceremony, used for millennia in diverse cultures, especially in the Andes, has its rules and rituals.

The principals of San Pedro are to support humanity and to recognize its low emotions or vibrations and raise them from neutral to a higher frequency. As humanity evolves, professionals and individuals are paying close attention to its benefits, and its popularity is coming back along with its teachings and practices. We can't forget that it is one of the oldest elements on this planet, and it is vital for the development of humanity.

San Pedro is being used as a medicine in many parts of the world today in conjunction with Western Medicine more times than you can imagine.

There are studies being done about the integration of San Pedro Medicine with Western Medicine, as well as with Shamanic Healing with Traditional Healing. The main focus of these studies is to show how they work together, while bringing fears, phobias and other pathologies to the surface. The integration of these two practices, along with the effect of San Pedro medicine, is to allow the person to perceive the subtlety of the messages.

Healthcare practitioners are most interested in how the San Pedro medicine is able to transmute and integrate any 'stuck situation' such as addiction, fears, attachments, etc. in the evolution of our being. Also, many healthcare providers see how much it helps directly with the integration of the heart and mind.

The rules of the San Pedro ceremony can be adjusted based on the Coordinator or Shaman's lineage and beliefs and how they choose to channel the medicine to assist you.

The following are some steps that may be used in a San Pedro ceremony:

The Ceremony has to be or should be in an open area, ideally around nature.
Area and participants should be cleansed.

San Pedro medicine should be taken by all participants together as a group. The Shaman and helpers usually don't drink but are at your service.

There should be a personal space for your journey. You are likely to experience a dream-like state in the first couple of hours. After that, you'll be more energetic and may feel like moving around.

Respect each other's privacy.
Limit the distractions to a minimum, as they may interfere with the healing process of others. If people need assistance, the Shaman or helpers will be there for them.

The Shaman and helpers will check on you from time to time and will do anything they can to make you comfortable.

Do not participate in songs or verbalize the words. This activity can also disturb others while they are going through their treatment and healing process.

Do not drink water during the ceremony, as it will dilute the medicine.

Some ceremonies have a MESA or an altar with various tools and protective talismans.
You can always bring fresh flowers for the MESA when applicable as well as amulets.

Integration will be part of the conclusion of the ceremony. Here you can share your experience, or not. There is no pressure to do this.

After the closing of the ceremony, you can relax, do whatever feels right, perhaps write a journal or go to bed.

DO NOT DRIVE after participating in a San Pedro ceremony. Plan ahead and have someone take you and pick you up from the location of the ceremony.

You go to a San Pedro ceremony with the intention of being in a sacred and safe environment. Take the time to explore and express yourself while working and understanding yourself in a conscious state. Target your fears and work through them and resolve them. You may also reveal to yourself a possible emotional trauma that you may have or have had in the past.

Be able to let go. Discharge whatever you do not need by cutting cords and vows you have made in this life or a past one which no longer serve you. You will be able to remove blocks that are holding you back from your goals, your happiness and from your life's purpose. This process of the ceremony will allow you to move away from the clutter and embrace your shadow, while letting you be your true and authentic self.

By believing in San Pedro medicine, you continue to learn and allow your heart to guide you while surrendering to your higher self. You will realize how important it is to align yourself with your thoughts and intentions. There is no separation from Source, only that which we create.

As part of Source, you will encounter the sensation of how much like home Source really is. You will feel pure love, humbleness and compassion. This state of abundance will allow you to dream and manifest what is for you, as part of your learning and growth on your journey.

This is why preparation, information and knowledge is so important prior to attending a ceremony so you can allow yourself to flow consciously, in total harmony, creating possibilities and new opportunities in your life.

SAN PEDRO CEREMONIES, AWARENESS & TEACHINGS

The beautiful San Pedro Plant Spirit medicine gives us the opportunity to experience things in such a profound and unusual way. We are always on the rational side of things and we are so structured, but we need to try and loosen up and be in touch with the other side as well.

Part of the preparedness for San Pedro Medicine is to practice both sides, in order to help us understand what will occur during the ceremony with the effects of the medicine.

San Pedro will do it for us. Yes, the medicine will lead us to be in touch with both sides while working with all of our senses. It makes us switch the focus of our awareness solely to our other side, for some time.

The Spirit of the medicine has the ability to lead us to go to areas that we do not look at, or we choose to ignore like traumas and deep emotions that we suppressed on our rational side. The medicine will lead us to solve or work on some of these issues for our overall wellbeing.

Besides showing us some painful and uncomfortable moments that we have been suppressing for a while, it will bring messages and solutions to help us resolve these problems and issues. This is why it is important to take these medicines without expectations and surrender ourselves to the healing process.

For these reasons, I love the medicine and the preparation process. In this way we will be ready to confront and allow whatever the medicine has in store for us as a treatment. When we are prepared and we have our conscious intention for the ceremony, we can work as a team with the medicine. The medicine will lead us to a state of happiness and bliss because it will open the path for healing. The medicine will show us a glimpse of how to make changes. It will be just a little tiny door that will open for us to see it and begin our work, evolvement and growth. This glimpse will show you the other side and provide you with possible solutions and understanding.

It is up to us to bring the information and the teachings into our journey. It is also up to us to 'take in' what San Pedro has for us and run with it.

Be responsible; take the information from San Pedro and do the WORK. Yes, you have to work the messages and the learnings, and go through the integration process and assimilation for you to fully understand what you have experienced in a ceremony. The Medicine will never completely solve a problem by itself without your participation and personal work. So, WORK and go for it!

San Pedro will bring awareness and teachings through nature. This information is rich and invaluable since we are going to be relating to nature during the ceremony. It shows us that we are not separated one form the other. San Pedro shows us both sides of us and of nature.

You will experience how a Flower is not just a Flower, Grass is not just Grass and a Tree is not just a Tree. The medicine shows us that, instead, there is an intelligence at work behind the scenes, behind a Flower, a Tree etc... It shows us how we can relate and talk to them and listen to their messages. These powerful moments are different and interpreted in many ways by each individual. In a very natural way, you will experience how many things we have in common with nature.

The beauty of working with Plant Spirit Medicine is the power that it has to show us how incredible our other side can be.

We will be able to understand more clearly how Mother Nature is always around us and connected to us . Everything is always interconnected in every moment. San Pedro makes us realize that looking at a field, a river or a tree is so much more than what our eyes perceive. When you are able to see the other side of nature, you will be able to relax and enjoy the beauty and their teachings from a very organic state.

Personally, I can say that nothing is separate. After my first experience with San Pedro Medicine, I changed my whole perception of the world, my life, routines and much more. After taking the medicine for the first time, I found it interesting how I was able to go back to my rational worldview. Nothing inside of me had changed but my views and perception had. I am now able to see a flower and feel it, sense it, and even listen to it while I'm on the other side of nature.

CHAPTER 5: AYAHUASCA

People who understand you without questioning or judging you are the ones who vibrate in a similar frequency....HF

HISTORY AND RELIGION

Ayahuasca has been around for many many years. This Plant Spirit Medicine has been utilized by the indigenous people in the Amazon dating back to at least, 2000 BC. However, the origin of Ayahuasca is not fully known. I will share some information with you that I found during my research.

There is evidence, based on archeological findings in the Southwestern area of Bolivia of Ayahuasca's presence. There is documentation that confirms that Christian missionaries from Spain found indigenous people utilizing Ayahuasca in what is currently Peru and Ecuador. This documentation dates from the 16th century.

Interest in Ayahuasca is fairly new in western medicine. Western scientists' investigations into Ayahuasca have only been documented over the last 150 years.

It is interesting to note that a British plant explorer discovered the Tukanoan Indians using a liana (a vine) known as caapi to induce a state of intoxication. These Indians were located in the Brazilian Amazon in 1851. (Richard Spruce)

More important historical information about Ayahuasca was found in 1858. Ecuadorian geographer, Villavicencio was exploring the jungle in Ecuador. He wrote very descriptive and specific comments about the medicinal plant. He described exactly where the plant was coming from and how the brew was utilized by the indigenous people. He proceeded to explain how the vine was used to foresee the future battle plans of the enemies, diagnose illnesses, determine which spells were used, and which ones to use, to welcome foreign travelers and ensure the love of their womenfolk. (Shultes, 1961) Villavicencio took the drink himself and later described the experience of 'flying to marvelous places.'

Although Ayahuasca is currently a banned substance in Brazil and most other countries, churches dedicated to the traditional use of it have sometimes been granted exemptions, as a nod to the significant religious affiliations associated with Ayahuasca.

AYAHUASCA & US LAW

Over the past 30 years, interest in Ayahuasca in the United States has grown from a simple curiosity to mainstream awareness.

Today, you can find Ayahuasca ceremonies with online advertisements, even though it is still illegal in the US. Unlike other illegal drugs, it is not viewed as addictive. Ayahuasca does not have the same negative stigma that LSD or hallucinogenic mushrooms have because it is a traditional Shamanic Medicine Ritual. There are important distinctions to make between

Ayahausca and other substances that contain the same hallucinogenic components.

Ayahuasca is a combination of two sacred plants: the Ayahuasca Vine (Banisteriopsis caapi) and a shrub known as Chacruna (Psychotria Viridis).

Ayahuasca is technically listed as a Schedule I controlled substance because it contains Dimethyltryptamine (DMT). The Drug Enforcement Agency (DEA) considers Ayahuasca to be equally controlled. Therefore, it is illegal in the US. Although Ayahuasca contains DMT, it differs due to its sacred use in Shamanic Medicine.

Throughout the country, you can easily find weekend Ayahuasca ceremonies. Some of these ceremonies will be small, underground ceremonial circles usually led by indigenous Shamans and non-indigenous trained healers. The number of followers varies, and a fee for participation is involved.

Ayahuasca ceremonies in the United States vary from Permitted to Prohibited, so, is it legal or not?

I will try to be brief and just give the basic information for you to understand its legality and when it is allowed. Only two main Brazilian Ayahuasca religions are permitted legally to use Ayahuasca. UDV (Uniao do Vegetal) and Santo Daime. Brazilian Ayahuasca religions are permitted to use Ayahuasca throughout the United States and Santo Daime can only be used in Oregon, California, Massachusetts, and The State Washington.

In 2006, the US Supreme Court granted the UDV permission to use the medicine in a seminal case on religious freedom. The Supreme Court ruled in favor of the group in an 8-0 decision, arguing that it was a violation of their religious rights. Thanks to this outcome, some religious groups are allowed to use it legally in their ceremonies. However, the UDV has to import and distribute Ayahuasca under the DEA's regulations. Anyone wishing to cultivate plants for the production of Ayahuasca must register with the DEA as a manufacturer of controlled substances.

Ayahuasca Healings and Soul Quest have submitted petitions for religious exemptions to the DEA, but have not received approval as of this writing.

Just be aware of the law and be cautious while enjoying the Ayahuasca ceremony.

WHAT IS DMT?

Let's try to understand what Ayahuasca contains and what DMT, often referred to as the 'spirit molecule' is all about.

DMT (N,N-Dimethyltryptamine), is a chemical substance that occurs in many plants and animals as well as Ayahuasca. It can produce the following effects:

- Auditory Hallucinations
- Euphoria
- Powerful Visuals
- Alteration in Sense of Time, Space and Body

It is true that people may be familiar with Ayahuasca these days, but not necessarily aware or familiar with DMT. It is a very strong psychedelic substance and can be produced synthetically, as well.

If an individual takes DMT orally, it doesn't become activated as a hallucinogenic without the inclusion of another substance. That's where Ayahuasca tea comes into the picture to make it effective.

It is important to know that DMT can be combined with various other substances to enhance the psychedelic effects.

In addition to using DMT in Ayahuasca tea, it can also be snorted or smoked. It can be injected but without the presence of certain alkaloids, it would have no effect.

It is important to be aware that when you take DMT as an Ayahausca tea it can have different effects on you. One of the effects is a rapid heartbeat, as I have mentioned before. This effect is one of the main reasons that some users have died drinking this tea. Other side effects include agitation, increased blood pressure, dilated pupils, chest pain, rapid eye movement and dizziness.

The effects are different depending on whether you are smoking DMT or drinking the Ayahausca tea. The difference is the length of the effect of the DMT.

It is also very important to know that taking DMT in high doses can lead to very serious side effects such as seizures and respiratory arrest.

It is not my intention in any way to frighten anyone who is going to attend a Plant Spirit Medicine ceremony. It is my intention though, to make sure you are informed and knowledgeable about the benefits, ingredients and their effects. You just need to be informed and responsible.

STREET NAMES
There are several alternative names for Ayahuasca, most of which are derivatives of the word, 'Ayahuasca', or refer to the plants that are used to make Ayahuasca, or the tribes that use this drug in religious ceremonies.
- Ayaguasca
- Quechua Ayawaska
- Lowaska
- Chacruna

- DMT
- Yage
- Mado
- Caapi
- Punga Huasca
- Daime
- Vegetal
- Hoasca
- Shillinto

AYAHUASCA AND THE BRAIN

Ayahuasca remains an unorthodox, psychological medicine in general, but this plant medicine is gaining more and more popularity and recognition worldwide, and is slowly working its way into the mainstream healthcare industry.

Not too long ago, if you wanted to experiment with Ayahuasca, you would have to travel to South or Central America. These days, it is easier to find ceremonies in the US and Europe.

As I have mentioned in many chapters of this book, indigenous people in countries such as Colombia, Brazil and Peru have been using the plant medicine for thousands of years; mostly for religious or spiritual purposes. These days, Ayahuasca tea is having a bit of momentum. It is coming to us more frequently through experienced providers such as Shamans.

The scientific evidence about the effects and benefits of the Ayahuasca brew is limited, but it is known to activate repressed memories in ways that allow people to come to a new understanding of their past. In some cases, the medicine can assist people to work through memories and traumatic events.

Today, neuroscientists are beginning to study Ayahuasca as possible treatment for depression and PTSD (Post Traumatic

Stress Disorder). In one study, 64% of Ayahuasca participants in a study reported significantly reduced symptoms of depression in one week after a single dose.

Remember, there are physical and psychological risks to taking it as well. It can interfere with medication and exacerbate existing psychiatric conditions, so let's get a little clinical, but not too clinical, and try to understand what happens to the brain when we take Ayahuasca. As we know already, the plant contains Psychotria Viridis and N, N-dimethyltryptamine (DMT). DMT is a substance that produces hallucinations and apparent expansion of consciousness. This is naturally in the plant.

DMT, N,N-dimethyltryptamine is a powerful hallucinogenic chemical that is considered a controlled substance in the US.

Let's understand that in our brain, we have DMT naturally as well. However, the plant itself has low bioavailability, meaning that it is a slowly absorbed drug by your physical body. However, DMT gets rapidly broken down by monoamine oxidases (MAOs) enzymes in the liver and gastrointestinal tract.

For this reason, DMT must be combined with another substance that containins MAO, monoamine oxidases inhibitors (MAOIs), which allows DMT to take effect. This way, the combination of these two will allow the body to absorb the medicine faster.

This is why Ayahausca brew contains Banisteriopsis Caapi, which contains potent monoamine oxidases (MAOs) which allows DMT to take effect. I believe that it is also important to mention that Caapi has a psychoactive effect of its own with messengers, or neurotransmitters that help regulate many bodily functions. Serotonin and dopamine have roles in sleep and memory, as well as metabolism and emotional well being.

MAOIs inhibit the degradation of neurotransmitters such as serotonin and dopamine. Let's remember that dopamine and serotonin are chemical messengers or neurotransmitters that help regulate many bodily functions.

In 2017, a study by Morales-Garcia suggested that the MAOI properties of Banisteriopsis Caapi stimulate neurogenesis in adults. Neurogenesis is the process by which new neurons are formed in the brain in the adult hippocampus. The hippocampus is a small, curved formation in the brain that is involved in the creation of new memories and is also associated with learning and emotions.

Some chemical studies were conducted on patients with treatment-resistant depression and found that a single Ayahuasca dose led to accelerated and long-lasting antidepressant effects. (Sanches, 2016)

There are many properties of Ayahuasca but the antidepressant properties of the Plant Spirit Medicine seems to be the one research that western medicine is taking the most interest in. There is strong evidence that the substance benefits patients with a variety of mental illnesses. More research is being conducted. There are over 100 articles in mental health journals exploring the benefits of Ayahuasca for eating disorders, substance abuse, PTSD and depression.

Additionally, Ayahuasca has also been found to stimulate neurogenesis, the process by which new neurons are formed in the brain and enhance creative thinking while decreasing conventional, convergent thinking.

If we want to summarize the effects of Ayahuasca in the brain, according to current research, we can say that Ayahuasca may protect brain cells and stimulate natural cell growth. Based on what I am able to present to you, we can also say that other benefits may include the ability to boost mood and improve mindfulness.

To confirm certain benefits like treatments for depression and addiction disorders, more research is needed, but many studies are being conducted even as we speak.

AYAHUASCA SIDE EFFECTS

Ayahuasca is a fantastic Plant Spirit Medicine when used by professionals or knowledgeable Shamans. The medicine, taken by mouth, has many effects on the human body. This is why it is so important to, not only prepare yourself for the ceremony but to do it with someone who has experience and knowledge, in order for you to have a positive outcome.

There are some serious side effects that a person may experience temporarily after taking the brew:

- Anxiety
- Diarrhea
- Nausea
- Panic
- Paranoia
- Vomiting
- Hallucinations
- Tremors
- Dilated Pupils
- Increased Blood Pressure

These side effects are common and some of them could be interpreted as part of your healing process, like purging and nausea symptoms. These unpleasant side effects are only temporary but they can be extremely distressing. It is very uncommon to have life-threatening side effects, but death has been linked to Ayahuasca use. Whether it was taken while under the care of an experienced Shaman or not, is not known. Some people have had miserable experiences with Ayahuasca. There is just no guarantee to what type of experience you may have.

Personally, I am saying that the medicine will lead you to the place on which you need to work. This is important for you to remember. Having a clear intention and being prepared for the ceremony will help you work with the medicine should you have an unpleasant side effect. You will be ready to go through it knowing how to benefit from it. You will know it because sub-consciously, you will remember what you are working on.

Ayahuasca can also interact with several medications, herbs and medical conditions.

You should NOT use Ayahuasca if you are taking the following:

• Anti-depressants, including Serotonin and tricyclic anti-depressants
• Cough medications, such as dextromethorphan
• Lithium or other psychiatric drugs
• Drugs used for Parkinson's Disease
• Methadone
• St. John's Wart
• Weight loss pills

Aside from these limitations and dangers, the benefits from participating in an Ayahuasca ceremony can be of tremendous help. Remember that you are putting your life in the Shaman's hands. You should trust the Shaman and research their knowledge and experience in working with the medicine. They are in charge of the ingredients of the medicine and the proper dosage. Part of their job is monitoring you for potentially life-threatening side effects as they guide you on your ceremony journey. Research the background of the Shaman or Coordinator.

If you are under a treatment for a psychological disorder, such as depression or PTSD, you should only take Ayahuasca while being monitored by a medical professional.

Even though many individuals feel that they received successful treatment from the medicine, more research is needed to establish whether Ayahuasca can be used for medical conditions by doctors in the future.

Those with a history of psychiatric disorders should avoid taking Ayahuasca. For example:

• Schizophrenia – Ayahuasca could worsen the psychiatric symptoms and cause Mania.
• Bi-polar Disorder-Ayahuasca might increase the risk of having a manic episode.

Beware: Pregnancy and Breast Feeding- Ayahuasca is LIKELY UNSAFE when taken by mouth. There is a concern that Ayahuasca might be toxic to the fetus is used during pregnancy. Avoid using.

CEREMONY AND EXPERIENCE
It is interesting to see how many people attend a plant spirit ceremony without the proper information or knowing what the ceremony is about. Many times, I will share with people that I am attending a ceremony and they will assume it is a wedding, when I say it's an Ayahuasca ceremony, they say, "oh yeah" but they don't have a clue as to what it's all about.

Usually, Ayahuasca ceremonies are held at night, but some are being done during the day. It is important to me to do it at night since the connection of the plant will lead you to your roots and your ancestors while opening your heart to work on personal issues and traumas. No interaction among the participants should be allowed.

The space where the ceremony is held will be prepared and blessed by the Shaman or Coordinator who is leading the ceremony.

You should bring specific items to the ceremony so you will be comfortable and ready to enjoy the travel with the Plant Spirit Medicine. There will be a short and intensive 5 to 6 hour period that will be spent in deep connection to a higher intelligence and an understanding of your true self. This is just the beginning. The medicine is very powerful and will lead you to work on the area that you need to concentrate on. It could be physically, emotionally or spiritually, connecting with ancestors, guides and Source.

Keep in mind that a typical Ayahuasca ceremony is a full night, and the effect of the medicine can last up to five hours, more or less. After consuming the medicine, most people start to feel its effects within 20 to 60 minutes.

I try to be very careful about how I describe my personal experience with the medicine because I do not want to be taken literally, nor do I want to mislead anyone about the effects or possible outcomes, since everyone is a beautiful, individual being, and we are all going to experience different things.

I can say that Ayahuasca can be like many years of therapy combined in just one download, or five years of therapy in one night. The idea of accepting and understanding issues, traumas and problems is what makes this medicine so successful for people with depression, for example.

Just think about this......If we are able to understand something, we do not need to create stressful thoughts. When we do not understand a situation, a loss, a divorce, or we have questions and obsessions involved in our behaviors, we are creating stressful situations, anxiety, anguish and frustration. So, when I experienced San Pedro and Ayahuasca, I was able to become more accepting of a specific situation or feeling, and I was able to move on to contentment and balance. I opened my heart, full of love and understanding, in a way that I had never done before. I think that what I just mentioned seems to be, more or less, an experience that many people go through during an Ayahuasca ceremony.

Another possible experience that you may have is being able to perceive everything through your five basic senses: seeing, hearing, tasting, smelling, and touching. Everything will be assimilated by your mind and will be deliberately created by the effect of the medicine rather than arising naturally or spontaneously. The organs associated with each sense will send information to the brain to help us understand and perceive the world around us. Just imagine how powerful this moment will be!

In my case, in one ceremony, after taking the medicine, I started to become super sensitive to sounds and vision. The sounds, at one point, felt so funny to me that I was laughing so hard, I was crying.

The physical and diet preparation is a must for me and I think everyone should do it. Doing this and going to the ceremony as pure and clean as possible will help you take full advantage of the medicine.
The plant will assist your body in discharging toxins and other chemicals such as sugar, salt, alcohol, caffeine. The great thing about it is, while you're preparing yourself for the ceremony, you will be cleaning and discharging toxins and impurities that you have accumulated over years. This is why PREPARATION IS SO IMPORTANT and you should commit yourself to the Plant Spirit Medicine from the moment you decide to be a part of the ceremony.
Do not be surprised if you purge or vomit during this time,

either during preparation or at the ceremony itself. Purging or vomiting may be part of your journey, and it can be very good if you need to do it. Make sure you bring a container for this purpose to the ceremony. Do not be concerned if you need to purge. It is normal and at times, expected. It's a great way to rid yourself of what is not needed in your body and in your journey. After purging, you may feel so peaceful and have a new outlook on what was apparently a dull reality. It is possible that the medicine allows you to shed and merge with the infinite 'other.'

Ayahuasca is always referred to in the feminine because users have said that the voice of higher intelligence that they hear during the ceremony is female. Ayahuasca is also known as the Grandmother of medicine. Many indigenous cultures considered Pachamama or Mother Earth to work through and with the Plant Spirit Medicine to help healing. In my research, I have also found that Ayahuasca was or is called the Mother or Queen of the medicinal plants by some Shamans.

As I mentioned before, this ceremony is traditionally done at night, preferably in a pitch black environment. Some theories say that the ceremony should be done at night to reflect the darkness of the roots going deeper into the earth; going deeper and deeper and darker and darker. These roots symbolize our ancestors and the indigenous tribes wanting to emulate the feeling of being in a dark womb. The womb was the first place where we were taken care of without requesting anything and where we were nurtured. It is the innocent pure child-state and our first connection with our mother before we entered this world.

The voice that you perceive and is heard by many people who have participated in the Ayahuasca ceremony speaks to you directly and tells you what you need to work on in your life. Remember, you may receive messages in many other forms, so do not sit and wait for the voice to call you.

One of the powerful moments for me is when the Shamans sing specific healing songs in their traditional language. The messages of the songs are so strong and can bring you healing fast and sweet. Paying attention to the songs is what allowed me to simplify my view on some of the problems that I was trying to resolve. Don't be surprised if you are able to understand other languages via a song. It is part of the medicine to remember previous lives and memories. You may have spoken one of the languages in a previous life. The Shaman or Coordinator will be the one who will initiate your journey for you and will be guiding you under the effect of the medicine.

It is important to understand that you may encounter some rituals and/or cleansings with tobacco or by other means. (I am getting emotional and excited just writing about it.) You can see how powerful the lessons from Ayahuasca are as they are still present in my mind. While having these thoughts and feelings, I am reconnecting with the spirit of the plant even as I am writing this. The Shaman may approach you and blow some tobacco to your crown chakra, heart, back and other places, so just go with the flow and enjoy the ceremony.

Remember that there is not just one way of conducting a ceremony. Every Shaman or Coordinator will follow his or her traditions and lineage. I suggest you ask him/her prior to the ceremony about what you can expect. This is why it is important that you know who will be leading the ceremony.

The importance of preparedness becomes more and more of a concern, since you will have an intense 4 to 5 hours of strong visuals and auditory hallucinogenic experiences due to the medicine and its main ingredient, DMT. The Ayahuasca plant is considered a visionary plant and by her spirit and vision, you can be healed. If you do not realize healing, at least you will be able to have a clearer understanding of what a better life is, through reaching various levels of consciousness.

Keep in mind that you may not be able to understand the whole healing process in a few days. The changes that this medicine provokes in you can be very intense and difficult to comprehend. Take your time, take small steps as you process, integrate and assimilate the outcomes.

CHAPTER 6: PSYCHOLOGICAL & MENTAL PREPARATION

Embrace your passion without fear to love....
Stop looking for a logical reason to love.... Let yourself flow
since you ARE love and you came into this world TO love....HF

SETTING GOALS
Setting goals is important, but more important is how we do it!
I was always setting up goals from a young age. That could be
good and bad at the same time. I realize that I have always been
a very goal oriented rational person.
It's ok to be ambitious, but make sure your goals are realistic
and grounded, while checking up on your ego and your greed.

I've been called a dreamer and many other names, as I ex-
plained in other chapters about not being understood. However, I've learned many things and have made many changes
during my 50 + years of life on this planet. My goals helped me
to achieve, manifest and gain many things, many of which were

not materialistic or superficial.

The truth is, having goals is knowing what you want and desire. One thing you should realize is that when you set up goals you should be easy on yourself. You need to be grounded when you set them up, so you will be sure that you have a sense of consciousness present at the time of goal-setting.

When you begin contemplating new goals, you should take a few minutes to really consider each question and answer yourself honestly, related to the goal that is going through your mind.

In the past, I've had many other things going through my mind, and I've since learned the importance of focus and clarity in order to reach what I want to achieve.

When I want to quiet my mind, I meditate for a few minutes with the intention of calming my mind and getting in touch with my inner-self. This way, I am able to find honest answers to all the questions going through my mind. This process of calming my mind and being brutally honest with myself, is the most important step I take to begin this change. Being honest, and as I said brutally honest, is a way of being direct and to the point without letting your ego or thoughts interfere with your true mission.

The importance of doing this step is that you are taking responsibility for your desires and actions. If you are able to do it, you will know at that moment if your goal is aligned with your true desire and intention. This quieting of the mind will assist you in seeing if the changes or the addition of new things, systems or behaviors that you want to implement in your routine will be successful or not.

You cannot begin a new project, healing process or even a treatment if you are not 100% clear on your desire and commitment. Taking the responsibility necessary is what will help you with this process to sustain, maintain and support you when you get discouraged.

Many people believe in the Law of Attraction. I do, as well, but this information that I'm sharing and expressing here is a combination of many laws, practices and techniques that I've learned throughout my training as a healthcare professional, educator and an energy and sound healer. Everything is inter-related and works with the same intention of assisting people to feel good and get their answers in a holistic and organic manner. You will discover your own system that works for you. There is not a specific system or technique to be used, but the intention of a goal and how you set it up, is.

My goal is to show individuals that there is not just one specific way to achieve or manifest a goal. Since it is very hard to change behaviors and/or new lifestyle changes, I believe that we should always try to be creative with a holistic approach while we can create a doable process.

The main goal is important, but it is more important to sustain those goals that are related or supportive of the main goal.

Once you have a clear desire, and you commit yourself to want to change a current situation, you can then take responsibility in the implementation and be able to move forward.

Just remember that every thought has energetic powers and vibration. The universe has observant and intelligent energies, and they will give you results to your wishes if you do them consciously.

Remember that a goal begins with a thought… so, make sure that your thoughts are done consciously, and results will come to you!

DETERMINATION

This journey has led me to many areas of enlightenment, while connecting and rediscovering myself on so many levels. The journey is way beyond what I was expecting to share with you. If you can relate to just one of the following synonyms of determination, you will be ready to begin your journey. Determination is mandatory to achieve and manifest your desires.

Determination: resolution, resolve, perseverance, persistence, resoluteness, backbone, single-mindedness, tenacity, courage, decision, purposefulness, steadfastness, stubbornness, boldness, decidedness, doggedness, obstinacy, staunchness, conviction, drive, energy, firmness, intentness, purpose, bravery, dedication, fortitude, indefatigability, pertinacity, strong-mindedness, tenaciousness, will power, braveness, constancy, grit, guts, inflexibility, nerve, obduracy, pluck, spunk, courageousness, granite, pluckiness, relentlessness, strength of character, certitude, dogmatism, intrepidity, staying power, assurance certainty, fearlessness, hardihood, sense of purpose, bulldog, spirit, self-confidence, strength of will, firmness of purpose, stickability, stick-to-it-iveness, stiff upper lip, stout-heartedness...

I am sure that you found a couple of words that resonated with you, correct? Good, because that is what you are going to need to continue your journey to Plant Spirit Medicine.

One of the things I learned while preparing for the Plant Spirit Medicine ceremony was that I had to build my spiritual strength as well as my physical strength. You have to exercise both of them, as this will facilitate the connection of your spirit to Source. The greatest outcome of these exercises is how it will lead you to a life of purpose and fulfillment. This will support positive thinking and will provide positive energy with happiness being the result.

Embracing, allowing and honoring yourself, your ancestors and your relationships is also a part of your preparation. It may be complex to understand when you start mixing and talking about all of them at the same time. Remember that you are part of Source and you are a beautiful human being. You need to see yourself in a holistic manner while you honor yourself to the fullest.

Take time to think beyond yourself and begin working on your relationships with others. Is there an area or situation that you would like to improve? Now is the time!

Feelings you have about your relationships and the impact they have on your emotional and vibrational state will reson-ate as frequencies in your being. These frequencies will then be represented in your thoughts. Thoughts have a significant impact on your life. Make sure that you do not hold on to nega-tive thoughts and memories that are not allowing you to move forward. Let them go, release them, and embrace today.

We come to this path to be happy and enjoy life. Allowing negative thoughts will take you away from that happy place. Your spiritual strength will be what helps you get back to a healthy and peaceful state of mind. So, take time to be with your family and friends and give those relationships the atten-tion and love they deserve.

Open your heart to Plant Spirit Medicine and your loved ones, while you allow the preparation and the medicine to work with you to build support for good relationships and positive thoughts. Tell your loved ones how much you appreciate them as you begin your healing journey.

As part of your determination in preparing yourself for the ceremony, you will find it is important to be in touch with nature. Respect the Earth and honor her live elements and ener-gies. Thank Earth for all she gives and recognize how little you do for her. Improve your connection with Earth and nature will support you with positive energy, flowing through your body and connecting you to Source. Try to engage with nature and begin to include activities that bond you with it. Take a walk on the beach, around the block, look at the moon, look at the sun and enjoy the sunshine on your face. Appreciate the experience with nature through your senses.

There is so much information and stimulation coming at you from all directions, and they can promote negative thoughts and create unbalance. Try to manage or reduce participation in these activities and stay focused on your path.

People, that know me personally, know my definition of happiness. For me, happiness is being able to maintain balance and peace in my life. Being able to have those two elements in my life and the opportunity to experience them, gives me strength to reconnect with Source and redirect myself with positive thoughts and, in turn, to positive energy.

Do we have control of our happiness? I think that we do, and we are responsible for how we support our own happiness; not just for a ceremony, but for our daily routine. Being determined to feel good and to be surrounded by positive energy is a choice!

Begin by choosing to be happy and to feel good. Be able to consciously become more humble and grateful while opening yourself up to positive energy. Receive it as well as give it out to others. Give it to the people who are sharing your space and your life.

Think twice when you feel the need to judge others and try not to give in to gossip. These things only waste your energy and create negative emotions.

In a Plant Spirit Medicine ceremony, I learned something that I carry with me every day. 'Do not concentrate on the pain or the sadness or the fear, as it does not serve anyone.'

That was a great learning moment for me and I adopted it as part of my routine to maintain my happiness. Focus on what makes you happy! Be kind to one another and try to see the good in all of the people that you interact with, even if they are being negative and interfering with your balance and peace.

I always think…."Who knows what they are going through in their lives that makes them so negative." If you keep your positive state of energy, this will not only be good for you, but will help them greatly as well.

There were times in my life when I thought I wasn't connected to Source because I didn't attend church on a regular basis, as was expected by the Catholic doctrine. I have learned through my evolvement and growth that I am a strong and confident person, and my vibrational relationship with Source has always been very strong.

I always knew that I was not alone. I knew that Source was guiding me in my darkest moments, even when my light was so dimmed, I realized that I was the one who had to blow those ashes away and bring back my fire. Once you realize that you are not alone and Source has your back, you can break through any challenges you may encounter. Go beyond your faith and welcome your teachers and guides and open yourself to a new beginning with Plant Spirit Medicine.

Sometimes, we don't realize how much good we can do with good intentions, love and humility. We may see the results and manifestation later on, surprisingly.

We are all part of Source and we are all connected somehow. Just remember who you are and what you want to be. The power is in your hands. Again, remember that every person you encounter is brought to you for a specific reason.

CLEAR DETERMINATION

Like everyone else, I am evolving and learning even as I write this chapter of the book. This is an unexpected chapter, but I need to use my gift as an educator. I was not planning to talk about this subject, but as I said before, I am being guided to tell you to be open to messages and to listen to your guides.

As I write this journey and begin sharing it with you, I have a lot of feelings that reappear as just memories and not as problems. I still feel them, and some of them are moving and confirming that I have learned my lesson from my last ceremony and the treatment selected by Plant Spirit Medicine was appropriate. Remember, the Plant Spirit Medicine will open the door to healing, but you must step through that door.

I am going to be brief, but I also feel I should clarify some terminology.

Determination is defined as a firm intent or decision which has been reached. An example of determination is continuing to apply for jobs after being turned down by dozens of potential employers. In my case, I was determined to find a medication free treatment for my acid reflux problem. My determination led me to research, create a diet and change habits which helped me to find the correct treatment and achieve my goal.

The meaning of determination is the act of coming to a decision or of fixing or settling a purpose.

We can define self-determination as a personal decision to do something or think a certain way. An example of self-determination is making the decision to go to a San Pedro or Ayahuasca ceremony without asking anyone's opinion.

It is important to keep in mind that demonstrating determination can be the key to success. Sometimes we need ways to be motivated and/or focus on the search of a treatment.

Clarify your focus. Take the time to determine what you are trying get to achieve in a very precise manner. Determined people know where they are trying to get, in detail. They cut to the chase. Determined people usually have a single goal they are focusing on.

Share your focus. Determination is the essence of increasing your chances of being successful in a particular thing or achieving a particular goal, as well as helping you to stay motivated and continue striving towards the one thing you want to achieve.

Just a note on determination: Determination is another important leadership trait. Determination is the desire to get the job done and includes characteristics such as initiative, persistence, dominance and drive.

Determination is a positive approach-related emotion, whereas anger is a negative approach-related emotion.

WANTS AND NEEDS

When you get to the point of thinking about what your wants and needs are, many things will go through your mind. It will be a moment of questioning yourself. When you begin the questioning or the discovery process, ask yourself if you are talking about your ego or your true wants and needs. I will not go too much into ego at this time, whether it is good or not. I am just going to say that we all have an ego and we will need to work with it.

But, in the case of wants and needs, this discussion will be related to the intention with regard to the Plant Spirit Medicine ceremony. Are we being realistic and what do we truly desire?

When I started thinking about attending a Plant Spirit Medicine ceremony, I knew that I wanted one thing primarily, but I wanted many other things, such as guidance and answers. I think that it is perfectly fine to want many things, but it is crucial to take the time to narrow it down.

Each of us will determine what we are looking for and what we think that we truly need. Think about what you want and if you truly need it. Many times we want things without needing them. It is not my place to tell you what you really need; it is based on what you believe, yourself. I will say that as part of your inner search and intention, it will be important to make a clear differentiation between what you want and what you need.

To give you more food for thought, I am providing you with some 'want' synonyms: wish, desire, demand, longing, yearning, fancy, craving and hankering. Some 'need' synonyms are: need, require, necessity, essential and requisite. Some clear cut examples of 'wants' are things like designer clothing, upscale dining, and sports cars. Without a doubt, these are luxury items and not necessities.

It is said that every person has unlimited 'wants' but limited resources. By this viewpoint, wants and needs can be understood as examples of the overall concept of demand. This is why I referred to 'ego' at the beginning of this chapter.

Let's just be very clear about 'needs' and 'wants.' Wants are desires for goods and services we would like to have but do not need. Many wants seem like needs.
Wants usually have a desire for possession or it's something we wish for. Needs refer to things we must have to survive, such as food, water and shelter. Needs are for essentials rather than just desirables.

Besides food, clothing and shelter, there are other basic needs like companionship, justice, free association, freedom, friends, family, work, religion and stable government.

Hopefully, now you have a better understanding of wants and needs. I just want to make sure that you are being true to yourself, and that what you are implementing into your life is really helping you, and not just making extra work and confusion. Therefore, when you write your intentions, be honest with yourself and ask if it is truly a need or a want.

EXPECTATION VS INTENTION
This is a subject that I was not going to talk about. However, after having a few conversations with some individuals, I decided to include it.

When I discussed this situation regarding the relevancy of an intention with many people, including Shamans and healers, their first reaction was to tell me they feel that when people participate in their ceremony, they like them to come without expectations. After listening to them, I realized that I still have my own opinion about this subject very organically. The truth of the matter is that there is a big difference between having expectations and having a clear, conscious intention for a ceremony.

It is not my goal to argue anyone's point of view or say who is right and who is wrong. I would just like to clarify how important it is to have a good conscious intention versus having an expectation of an outcome.

Nowhere in this book does it say that we should expect anything specific from the Plant Spirit Medicine, nor does it say that the medicine will work in such and such a way or a specific manner. This is just one of the reasons why we cannot go to a ceremony with expectations, since the medicine will be the thing that will guide you to where the spirit of the plant feels that you need to go.

However, I do firmly believe that for us to be able to take advantage of or benefit from a ceremony, especially if we want to work on a specific issue or trauma that we have already identified, we should have a clear intention.

This intention should be consciously arrived at during the preparation process. The intention will carry over through all of the steps and that is just the beginning. You will understand why I am saying this as you are participating in the ceremony. The medicine will show you and take you to other areas that you were not considering as an issue. The spirit of the medicine will guide you through these issues while healing them and supporting your initial intention, either directly or indirectly.

Here we go with the definitions.....

Intention: Intention is your goal, your purpose or aim. It's something that you mean to do, whether you pull it off or not. Some common synonyms are: design, end, goal, intent, objective, purpose.

Just remember that a person's intentions are important, but if nothing is done, then the intention doesn't really matter. In this case, it will matter because the intention is the idea that your plan will be carried out through your ceremony participation.

Go for the experience, without expectations, while surrendering and allowing the medicine to guide you and provide healing treatments.

Expectation: Expectation, on the other hand, is the act or the state of waiting for something you think will happen; to wait in expectation. It is really the act of looking forward or anticipating an outcome.
For example: If you are going to a ceremony with an ex-

pectation, it is because you are HOPING that something will happen, so, if you are going to participate in a ceremony because you are trying to heal a specific ailment, and you think that by the end of the ceremony, you will be healed, that is an EXPECTATION. It is an expectation because you are waiting for that outcome and that specific result.

We can also say that expectations come from an EGO state that is attached to or identified by the outcome. Think about that! Also, here is where we get disillusioned because it may not meet or measure up to the outcome that you expected or thought or dreamed.

Are expectations bad for us to have? The negative effect of expectations is that you give your trust to someone or something. It's like putting all your faith in something that is not real. Keep in mind that if an expectation fails, whether it is placed on other people, an event, or even yourself, it's going to hurt. You will be disappointed, have angry feelings and feel frustrated.

Today, during this pandemic, many people had projected many expectations for their journey and personal life. In many cases, these expectations remained unmet. Expectations about the future can create depression, anxiety and feelings of inadequacy, impatience and hopelessness. Just think about it. If you didn't have expectations, everything would become so simple. You would simply take things as they come and deal with them.

Without expectations, acceptance of what is would be so much easier!

DESIRE, INTENTION AND DECISION

We use words during many moments of our journey without giving them their power and importance. Most interestingly, we forget the powerful vibration that each word possesses. Depending on how we pronounce them and what power and conviction we give to them when we speak them, their vibration will affect us. Let's look into the words; desire, intention and decision and try to understand how these words resonate with us and their true meaning.

I am going to concentrate on words that we use or feelings that we experience because all of these words will be involved with a thought that is powerful and they need to be controlled. Let's understand desire, intention and decision and how they differ from each other.

The definition of desire is a strong feeling of wanting to have something or wishing for something to happen. The desire will come from within us as just simply, what we truly desire.

Just recall why you began thinking about doing a San Pedro ceremony. Maybe, it was because you wanted to find a cure for something or find balance or even guidance from Source. It's something uncertain and a wish, without knowing if you will accomplish that wish.
An intention, on the other hand, really involves acknowledging the desire while leaving it free and in the present moment. This way, the intention will take the appropriate path or action that is aligned with your desire.

In this case, when you decide to attend a Plant Spirit Medicine ceremony, you create an intention, a conscious intention with the ultimate goal of achieving manifestation. This process has a deeper inner search that will lead you to believe that it is possible, but, the truth of the matter is, at this time, you are just wishing for something that was not manifested yet.

If you understand the origin of where the feeling comes from, it will help you to understand that the desire comes from a place of 'Yes, yes, it would be nice to have that.' In this case, it is more like a wish and there is no guarantee that you will get what you wish for. For example, it's like when you are on a diet and you are craving something. Most of your desires come from lack of fear. Just think about it. When you're eating that piece of cake that you desire, and it's not part of your diet, fear is not present at that moment and you just go for it. Your desire is stronger than your fear. Get it?

On the other hand, intention is stronger than desire. If you put your mind to something and do it consciously, like preparing for the Plant Spirit Medicine ceremony and researching and acquiring information about it as you are doing it.

When you select this position regarding your decision, it is more likely that you will accomplish something if you intend to do it, rather than, just have a desire to do it. Note: Remember that it can still be influenced by desire or your ego.

Now, decision....how powerful is decision and when should we consider decision?
Decision is more powerful than intention or desire. When we take this position in making a decision, there is no uncertainty whatsoever. When we make a plain and simple decision, it is done! Just like after your search, your readings and findings, you decide to attend a Plant Spirit Medicine ceremony...just go for it!

A decision comes from a very deep inner place of our being and will be like a fact that you truly believe in.

Because your decision is a fact for you does not necessarily mean it is a true fact for someone else or even a true fact at all.

CHAPTER 7: THE INTENTION

Wake up each morning with the intention of loving each moment....because you ARE love and you came to this planet searching for that love that is within you....HF

THE INTENTION

Intention, Intention, Intention. With these three words comes Manifestation, Manifestation, Manifestation!, but, do we really have any idea about how important it is to create a proper intention?

We all want results and manifestations while reaching our goals and objectives. We want the crystallization of our ideas that we create or think that we create. Sometimes, we just don't realize how simple this can be, if we just align ourselves with our intention and desires organically. Organically, meaning naturally and something that just flows.

Society creates myths about what happiness really is. It makes us believe that if we achieve and we accumulate material things, we are being successful on our journey. 'The more the better' is society's idea of success and happiness. It takes much more than material things for a person to be successful and happy.

So, what is success? I am not trying to create a debate or be a motivational speaker at this time. However, I think it's important for everyone to understand and define success and happiness. I would like to give my opinion in regard to the definition of success. As a goal oriented and rational person, I have learned that acquiring money does not mean you are successful, nor is it a guarantee of happiness. Success is when you enjoy every step taken toward a specific goal.

Many individuals concentrate on the finish line and end result. These people do not enjoy the process, and they eventually realize that reaching that particular goal did not give them pleasure or satisfaction.

Even if the goal is to make money or acquire something tangible, the process taken to reach that goal must be enjoyed and should contribute to the learning and evolving process, even if there are problems along the way. The idea is to feel good even if there are ups and downs. The joy and the passion of trying to overcome problems is part of the experience of learning as we get closer to that ultimate goal.

Part of my learning in Plant Spirit Medicine ceremonies was to remember things that I took for granted or hadn't taken into consideration. Even though I had a clear intention of healing my heart and sorrow, the medicine had some other areas that it wanted me to work on as part of my healing and treatment. The medicine needed to show me so much more than what I was looking for with my intention.

The power of the medicine will take you to places that you must become aware of in order to continue evolving and learning about yourself, your gifts and who you truly are.

The Plant Spirit Medicine reminded me, that after 50 years on this path, I have already accomplished many goals and evolved in a lot of areas. The medicine made me realize many things. Somehow, I am now remembering why and how I was able to achieve what I have already achieved. I am receiving details of messages about the important steps that I took for the materialization of those ideas, desires and goals in a very natural and organic way.

If we believe in the power of the universe and the power of Source, we can agree that those two things have a lot of power over us as individuals. The higher powers possess energy intelligence and can give us what we want as a result. In understanding these properties of the higher powers, it will be easier for us to recognize them when we receive them.

The second and most important step in achieving the results you want will involve the way in which you are doing it. You must do it in a state of consciousness. If you do not do it consciously, you will not be able to send your vibrating energies to the universe and the results will never be achieved. Results will never materialize because you will not be connecting with the universe's intelligence energies. If the universe can observe your energies, that proves that the energies have intelligence, doesn't it? If we do not set our intention in a conscious manner, you will not be able to send those true messages to Source and the universe.

SYNCHRONIZE YOUR THOUGHTS WITH YOUR FEELINGS. DON'T JUST THINK IT…. FEEL IT!

As an innovator of many businesses, I have heard people say, "Why is it that every time I want to start my own business, something happens?" or "Why can't I manifest an idea and put it to work?" or "Why can't I stay on a diet?" or "Why can't I forget about a situation that is still causing me pain?"

I am very much into seeing people manifest their desires, and I have helped many individuals and corporations achieve their manifestation goals. In the course of my career, I realize that the secret to manifesting a desire, whether in business or just in daily life, is all about a clear and defined intention. You cannot reach the manifestation level until you understand what you truly want, consciously.

Having an idea or a thought does not mean that you have a clear intention or know how to resolve a situation or a problem. An idea begins with a desire and that desire must have a very clear intention. You need to understand and remind yourself that you are part of and connected to Source, energies and the universe. They are always teaching us. As part of this association, you also have a connection with your vibration that will emanate your desires through energy.

The Plant Spirit Medicine preparation and the medicine itself reminded me of the power of our thoughts. From the time I was deciding why I wanted to participate in a ceremony, or why I believed that this medicine was what I needed to correct my problem, I had to control my thoughts and my emotions. I had to be consciously aware of what my clear objective and intention was. Being able to control those thoughts allowed me to be clear in my intention. I knew that I wanted to heal my heart, but I also knew that I had to change patterns and align my emotions with Subconscious and Conscious. That thought alone, was a lot!

While I was sorting thoughts and understanding their powers at the ceremony, I realized I needed to leave the drama aside. I was able to do it because I had a clear, conscious written intention before I attended the ceremony, and it allowed me to understand what the guides were telling me under the influence of the medicine. The drama that I was creating in my mind was not allowing me to let go of my pain and start the healing process. If I had not had the conscious and written intention, I would not have been able to assimilate or understand what the guides were telling me as easily as I did. I believe it was because I already knew my intention consciously, and under the medicine, I had no resistance from my ego or my fears. I was able to see what was presented to me and its correlation to my issue. Everything works as a team and in conjunction with your intention very holistically.

For the past six months, the words consciously and consciousness have been in my mind and in my writings, my speeches and in everything I do. I totally understand the message now after a Plant Spirit Medicine ceremony. It allowed me to see how important it was for me to accept myself and be open to receive consciously.

It especially allowed me to be in touch with my feminine side and become more open and receiving. I needed to learn consciously to not always be the one who is giving. It was time to balance myself and open myself to receiving as well. As I am writing this chapter, I also realize that by opening my receiving channel, I was opening myself to getting more messages and support from the healing medicine.

I know I say this a lot, but if we do not set an intention or act consciously on the things we desire, we will not see results. This is why so many people are not able to reach a level of manifestation. Therefore, if you want to receive something and you desire to manifest the results for your desires consciously, the vibrations and energies will reach the universe and return to you to conclude the manifestation process and solution.

The art of manifestation comes with the art of allowing, as well. I will allow my desire, with my intention, freely while welcoming everything that comes with it. Being able to receive and welcome what it comes with, is the key to evolving and expanding ones learning process.

When we talk about allowing or the art of allowing, you are able to flow and receive all the teachings that will come to you during the process. This means you should allow the good with the bad, as part of the lesson to be learned, as it helps you to grow and evolve.

Many times an idea is just an idea. We think that we have a great business idea but it is really not well thought out, and we start making mistakes while we allow our ego to take over without being grounded and setting a clear intention.

Once you get an idea of what you want, you should take the time to truly ask yourself, "How much do I believe in this idea?" "Do I really want it to be manifested?" "Do I really want to commit myself to investing time and energy into it?" "Am I truly ready, consciously?" These questions could be considered 'ego interference,' but, I believe it is necessary for the simple reason that you have to make sure it is what you want, and also that you're not doubting yourself. The reason for these questions is to prevent any type of disappointment in the future. One more question, 'Is your desire realistic?'

While I was writing, I received a message from my guides for the readers, and even though I was not going to talk about this, my guides and angels are telling me the following. I will write it exactly the way that it came to me since I want you to feel a raw message without editing.

"Being able to observe....generates immortality in a situation....the thought maintains its power....will activate in the DNA of the soul....in the quantum level of things....the universe, Source, the higher powers with their intelligence energy fields and their sensitivity of being observed....will allow you to know how to observe....if you don't know how to observe, you will not be able to get a response....if you do observe consciously, it will generate an intelligent wave to things and the things will respond....if you don't know how to observe, you will be using a tool without knowing how to use it and there will be no result."

You also need to know that intelligent forces will respond to names. Consciousness needs to be present in order to manifest. Call things by their names, consciously and with determination, knowing exactly what you want and what you desire. Be specific and don't waste your energy.

Having this information is what really made me understand the importance of preparing oneself for a ceremony or event. At this point, you can now see how preparing yourself for the Plant Spirit Medicine ceremony is a learning journey, not only for your soul and healing process, but for your daily life with an organic and holistic approach.

I believe that my purpose and intention with this book is not just to be able to share messages and experiences, but to be able to give clues and guide others with the information that worked for me. I am transforming my life with this information and I know you are going to do the same.

Somehow, we are both looking for happiness, balance and healing. We believe in instruction and learning as we are evolving, and as you are reading this last line consciously.

WRITING YOUR INTENTION

I would like to begin by saying that I am not an expert on anything, and it is not my intention to become one. I will continue to allow the information that is flowing through me to continue without resistance. I had not really planned on writing this chapter, but I feel that my guides want me to do so. It is very special to be able to share with you my current feelings, emotions and vibrations while manifesting this book. It is my pure, personal pleasure.

I will try my best to describe to you how it feels receiving a message and how to welcome it and surrender to what you are receiving.

Everything begins with an intention, and this book is not an exception. My intention is focused on how to transmit my journey and experiences through my writing, thoughts, messages and information that I receive and continue to receive.

I know that it is not an easy task to transcribe feelings, thoughts and messages in a tangible form such as this book. I have been blessed to have an editor, Cindy VanDusen on my path. She is not only my editor, but my friend, and surely a mother or relevant person in my past lives. She is able to understand me, my train of thought and my messages, as well as my accent for the past 15 years or more.

She works for me in many of my businesses, and she was able to experience, first hand, some of my predictions, manifestations and messages received throughout our time together. She accompanied me and supported me going way back to my first love, singing. When she first heard me sing, I was partially retired from performing. We share a very similar vibration when we are together, and we can tune in to each other within seconds. Somehow, she gets my thoughts, running so fast through my brain, and even when I verbalize them with my accent. I feel sympathy for her but somehow, she does it, and I am grateful and humble.

Prior to working on this journey with Cindy, we had many conversations for hours, during several days and weeks and we concurred that our intention for the editing of this book was to be as organic and holistic as possible. From the time I presented her with this project and invited her to walk this journey with me, we were able to relive many wonderful experiences. Throughout the project, she would call and tell me how she realized that I had been doing this since she first knew me, without having any idea that I was doing it. Other times, she would call me and tell me that messages were flowing and resonating with her while she was reading them during the editing process.

As you can see, our intention was not to generate money or fame. Our intention was not even to produce a book. (We already had that experience and we even won an award). That was ten years ago. Our intention here was to deliver messages and share experiences in order to prepare you for a Plant Spirit Medicine ceremony.

Now, I am being told by my guides to help you write your intention. Please don't feel that I am underestimating your knowledge and your experience, but I am being told to do so, and I will continue flowing with my journey.

Remember that readers, including myself, are all evolving at different times. What is redundant for you may be beneficial for others. We will practice unconditional love and patience, and we will all learn from it as well.

As part of this chapter, I will give you examples, based on my knowledge and experiences. I will be basing this on a question that I usually ask my participants at one of my weekly seminars. "What is Happiness for You?"

From the moment I realized that I needed to change things, such as behavior and my approach to new events, I began asking myself, "What makes me happy?" "What is happiness for Humberto?" This question became relevant when I was in a dark place with no light to follow. As I realized that my light was not completely out yet, I knew that I needed to take responsibility and control of my situation. I understood that I had to be the one to make that light become brighter.

The first step I take when I begin with a new group is to determine what happiness is for each of them, because each of us has a different definition of happiness. Never the less, at the end of the day, we are all trying to find peace and balance. We are always searching for that, 'feel good sensation' because we do not come to this journey to suffer. We travel this path to learn, evolve and be happy.

It is interesting to see how individuals base their happiness on events, people and material things. Almost 90% of the time, people base their happiness on events.

For example, people will say:
Happiness is when I'm camping with my children
Happiness is when I'm surrounded by my family
Happiness is when I am singing
Happiness is when I am sleeping or meditating
Happiness is when I am in a relationship
I am sure that you can relate to many of these sentences, but let's take it a little further. We are all talking about events. It is important to determine what type of feeling these events generate in you. What type of emotions do you experience? Also, how do you feel those emotions? Are you consciously feeling those emotions? Are you able to re-create them when you want them or need them? Can you re-create those feelings on your own? Can you make yourself happy? If you need to do it today, at this moment, can you re-create that feeling? Are you in control of your happiness?

All of these questions are part of your own discovery, so when you need to write an intention, you need to be very honest and know yourself very well. The intention must be true and organic and in this case, when you write your intention, you MUST vibrate to it.

One day, I told my teacher about my feelings concerning intentions. When we go to different types of spiritual circles, we have to express our intentions and I often feel that members do not have a defined intention. Their intentions are too broad and not thought through well enough. I am not saying or criticizing that 'broad intentions' are not good or consciously created. But, when you go to a Plant Spirit Medicine ceremony, you should really know what or where the pain is and what is causing it in order to resolve it. The medicine will give you the treatment and much more than you are asking for, but you need to work with the medicine as a team to get your desired results.

When you write an intention consciously, your vibration will communicate with the universe, Source or higher power and results will be given to you.

Why is it more important to have a very definite intention when you go to a specific event such as San Pedro or Ayahuasca? It is important because, in this case, we are searching for a healing treatment. We are participating in an alternative medicine treatment by our own choice. We are not going to a doctor for medication or to follow his recommendations. We are choosing an alternative method that we believe in and are willing to work with the medicine to achieve our goal.

I am sure you researched this method before going to a ceremony. This is why you are reading this book. You are doing research and preparing yourself for a ceremony. It is not coincidental that I needed to write this book for you.. Messages come in mysterious ways. You need to prepare yourself for them, as well as for the ceremonies and events that you consciously choose to participate in and attend.

Going back to my group examples that I mentioned before, and their answers as to what happiness is for them, I asked them to take a few moments and close their eyes and truly try to go deeper within their emotions. It is important to do this process in order to discover the true feelings that were making them feel so good. Once they did that, then they needed to question themselves or try to understand how to feel that again. The good thing is that now they know that a feeling was the generator of feeling good. If it was a feeling or an emotion that they were encountering, that means they had control of it.

Let's continue....
So far, the first step is to determine what happiness is for each one of us. Secondly, we close our eyes and go deeper to recognize the feeling that the event provoked in us. Thirdly, is to look into the types of feelings you were able to experience in this discovery.

I suggest you write these steps down. When you are able to see them in writing, they become more powerful. Finding the true meaning of happiness for yourself is finding your self-purpose. Always remember, you come to this path not to suffer, but to feel good.

Now that you were able to determine one or two true feelings that make you happy and feel good, how can you reach those feelings without being in an event? It is important to find a way to reach those feelings and work on them. This is how you look for true results and prepare yourself for the Plant Spirit Medicine.

Let me give you an example. I am hearing that I need to tell you about my experience, and this way, you will be able to grasp it better. Here I go....

When I went to my last Plant Spirit Medicine ceremony, I already knew the steps and what to expect. I was ready. I truly prepared myself for the healing of my current situation. I chose to go to the ceremony. The ceremony also came to me. I was not aware that a ceremony was happening. It was just brought to my attention by a colleague, and I hadn't told anyone that I was looking for it at the time.

Because I know and believe that being prepared and ready is important, I began with my physical and spiritual preparation as soon as I decided to attend. This information that I am sharing with you came from colleagues and teachers. I am not inventing anything, nor am I creating anything that was not created before. I am just delivering messages, as I have said before.

My first step was to think deeply about why I chose a Plant Spirit Medicine ceremony. Right away, I started thinking about why I wanted to do it and what issues I wanted to work on. My intention was clear that I wanted to work on myself and allow myself to receive messages and get the healing I was looking for. But, as you can tell, this was a very broad intention, so, I began to go deeper to see what my true intention really was going to be at the ceremony.

I did the same steps that I mentioned before. I knew what happiness was for me. I knew that peace and balance were the two items that composed that happiness. I wanted to be very clear and conscious of my intention for the ceremony. I closed my eyes and started going deeper and deeper within my thoughts and feelings to determine what my true intention for the medicine was. At this time, I had to really take control of my thoughts, ego and fears to achieve what I wanted. YOU CAN DO THIS!

I was able to narrow the searching down to a specific intention for the ceremony. I went with the intention of healing my broken heart from a life experience that I had recently gone through, on my journey. Even though I was looking for 25 million other answers in 25 million other places, I searched my soul and realized that I wanted to feel good. I needed to work on myself and find healing for my heart so I could begin a new path with peace, balance, humility and gratefulness.

Narrowing down your intention to one specific thing does not mean that you won't get other messages as well. What it means is that your primary issue will be your target, consciously and will be your focus when you get to the ceremony. In a way, it's like understanding that you are in control and you will do the work that is needed, with the assistance of the medicine and together, you will be able to find the treatment that will lead you to healing and happiness.

Understand that this is not easy and it may take more than one ceremony to achieve your ultimate goal. The first time I went, I received so much information that I was not able to absorb it all. You need to keep working on yourself on different levels in order to achieve your evolvement.

I think it is wise and respectful on our end to allow the medicine to help us. We are always healing ourselves and it is fine and beautiful, but we also need to learn how to take advantage of this beautiful plant medicine while working with our guides and teachers.

The beauty of this medicine is that it will guide you with your narrowed, conscious intention during the ceremony. Pay attention to what the medicine is telling you.

While you are under the effects of the medicine, you will be conscious but your subconscious will also be present and that is the beauty of it. I call it the 'meeting of the subconscious and conscious.' I am not a doctor or a psychologist, but I was able to work on my intention with the medicine and the presence, of my guides and archangels while allowing myself to see and feel the suggestions from my guides without barriers or fears.

It is so important for you to know why you are choosing to do this ceremony, and what your true intention is. Remember, you will also get answers to many other questions or thoughts that you have during the 12 to 15 hour ceremony.

I cannot stress enough the importance of being prepared and having a clear intention before attending a ceremony, so, next time you attend one, prepare yourself as I have told you throughout this book. Prepare physically, spiritually, emotionally and mentally.

While it is best to prepare yourself before going to a ceremony, it is still alright to go without having a specific intention, as the medicine will still give you an experience that you need. There is no right or wrong, and the experience will still be amazing and may be useful as part of your discovery.

The intention of this chapter is for everyone to understand that we DO have control of our actions. We DO have control over how we approach a new event. We DO have control of our intentions when done consciously. We DO have control when we are looking for healing and treatment. We DO have control of our happiness.

CHAPTER 8: THE PHYSICAL PREPARATION

Stop the negativity in your life....
It is very simple to do.....
Just stop talking about it...HF

DIETARY RELEVANCE

Diet or DIETA is a large part of the commitment to a Plant Spirit Medicine ceremony. The purpose of doing a specific diet or DIETA is to prepare yourself and generate a good connection with the medicine. The dietary preparation can have a very beneficial effect. Personally, I do a minimum of 10 days of dieting. This is what I was taught at my first ceremony. I believe that commitment, dedication and honoring the spirit medicine is a must. I love the idea of beginning the healing process from the moment I decide to attend the ceremony. While taking this personal position toward the medicine, I begin tuning myself with the medicine and its vibration.

If you think that 10 days is too long, or you may not be able to do it, I suggest you do it for at least 3 days prior to the ceremony.

Food and drink should be as simple as possible as part of your conscious preparation, and it will be a great support for your intention at the ceremony. If you follow the guidelines and a clean diet, it will provide the best conditions for the Plant Spirit Medicine to work within your system.

Do not stress about the diet. Just focus on keeping your diet as clean as possible. The purer your body and spirit are, the more powerful the medicine and its teachings.

So that we truly understand what DIETA is, it does not just refer to food and drink restrictions. The DIETA is proposed and observed as part of the process of taking the medicine with a pure intent. For many cultures, DIETA is a change of lifestyle and should be carried on long after the ceremony, as part of our daily routine.

Cleansing the body in this way is ceremonial and practical. While removing toxins and heavy food from the body, it allows the medicine to be absorbed more easily and work deeper. You want to make sure that you work with the medicine and not against it.

DIETA
DIETA is the Spanish Word for diet. The purpose of the DIETA is to connect deeply with a specific plant, either for healing or as a form of initiation, but usually, for both.

Each Plant Spirit Medicine will have its own specific restrictions. Your Coordinator may have his/her own DIETA plan. Be sure to ask them before the ceremony if they have their own diet plan for you to follow.

The dietary and lifestyle restrictions will allow you to work deeper and more effectively. This will allow the Plant Spirit Medicine to have a stronger effect on your body. Picture that the plant is growing inside you, and you will be benefitting from its wisdom and healing power.

If you begin the process prior to attending a ceremony, and you believe in the Plant Spirit Medicine, your healing treatment will begin from the moment you start the DIETA. At least, that's the way it is for me. The reason I am writing this is so that you will be able to benefit from this process as much as I did, and will continue to do so.

When you do the DIETA in preparation for the ceremony, you will be clearing your body of toxins, habits, stagnation and bad energies. Shamans usually recommend this DIETA a few weeks or a few days before the ceremony.

I, personally recommend being on the DIETA, without cheating, for 10 days minimum prior to the ceremony.

I see the DIETA process, as a discovery process, and one you should enter into with the plant spirit and yourself. The process will reveal insights about you and to you. You should enjoy, embrace, learn and listen to yourself with your body, mind and soul. This is a perfect time to connect to the plant spirit and Source.

Part of the DIETA teaching is that when you are preparing for the ceremony, your diet should be aligned with your behaviors. It is now that your actions and your eating will be working together with the same intention. You should be making your body as free of toxins and chemicals as you possibly can. Remember, DIETA will require effort and dedication in order to work well.

If you are working with your ceremony intention along with the DIETA, and you live it in mind and body, it will become real at the ceremony.

TRY NOT TO CHEAT. Remember, it is a relationship, after all.

As important as the DIETA is, you should consult with your Shaman or Physician before doing it. The same is true of taking the Plant Spirit Medicine.

Some of the illnesses that can be affected by the medicine are:
- Colon Problems
- Atrial Fibrillation (rapid heartbeat)
- High Blood Pressure
- Diabetes
- Mental Illness

Even if one of these is the reason you are taking the Plant Spirit Medicine, your Shaman or Physician should be consulted for your safety.

FASTING

Fasting is the willful refrainment from eating for a period of time. The purpose of fasting is not to suffer. Fasting is to guard against gluttony, impure thoughts, deeds and words. Fasting must always be accompanied by prayer and almsgiving (donating to a charity or directly to the poor, depending on circumstances).

I adopted fasting as part of my daily routine. Monday through Friday, I do intermittent fasting which allows 8 hours for eating and 16 hours for fasting. I do this type of fasting two to three times a week. This really works for me, and makes me feel so much better. It makes my energy levels soar, and I feel highly productive. As I always say, I am not an expert on anything, and I am just sharing what works for me.

Based on my research, here is a list of the health benefits of fasting:

- Promotes blood sugar control by reducing insulin resistance
- Promotes better health by fighting inflammation
- May enhance heart health by improving blood pressure, triglycerides and cholesterol levels
- May boost brain function and prevent neurodegenerative disorders
- Aids weight loss by limiting calorie intake and boosting metabolism
- Increases growth hormone secretion which is vital for growth, metabolism, weight loss and muscle strength
- Could delay aging and extend longevity
- May aid in cancer prevention and increase the effectiveness of chemotherapy

There are also psychological benefits to fasting. Think about fasting like a period of profound rest. At this time, your body is free to rapidly undertake a wide variety of beneficial physiological activities like 'neuroadaptation', since fasting will help your taste sensors adapt to a low salt intake, which will facilitate the adoption of a health-promoting diet.

During fasting, your body induces enzymatic changes that can affect numerous systems, ranging from detoxification, mobilization of fat, glycogen and protein reserves. The positive side of these changes is that they continue after the fasting process.

Fasting is not recommended as a primary weight loss plan. This will happen automatically during the fasting process due to the limitation of calories along with a cleaner diet.

For me, personally, detoxification is the objective of fasting. Fasting facilitates detoxification, promoting the mobilization and elimination of substances created in our system, such as cholesterol, uric acid, and toxic chemical residue.

Based on research, fasting appears to have a profound effect on insulin resistance involving diabetes and high blood pressure issues.

You can also reduce 'gut leakage' that is usually associated with arthritis, colitis, asthma, allergies and fatigue.

If fasting resonates with you, please feel free to do more research and educate yourself on finding the benefits that match your goals. Always consult your physician before a fasting procedure.

WATER FASTING
Since the beginning of this century, medical innovation and advancement occurred from radiation therapy to self-healing techniques like water only fasting. These were largely unappreciated.

The beauty of these types of evolvement in our society was the realization that health and healing work best when they are natural processes. This is one of the ways that the shift began from traditional or western medicine with a concentration on drugs and surgeries, toward moving to a more natural process of healing.

We can recognize that the majority of today's health problems is the result of modern dietary excess. I always remember a song from 'Queen,' one of my favorite bands. It was called, 'Too Much Love Can Kill You.' Simply put, most of our health problems are the result of our getting too much of the wrong things. We just need to be balanced and know what can hurt us even if it tastes like LOVE.

Current societies ingest too much animal fat and protein, as well as refined sugar and carbohydrates. The use of drugs, tobacco, coffee, and soda also contribute to poor health. It is important for us to take control of our diet and our lifestyle.

As the world is going through so many unprecedented epidemics of disease, many people are paying attention to the ancient healing method of water only fasting. This type of fasting is beginning to make intuitive sense to many people. Understanding and implementing water fasting is transformative for many of us.

Water fasting has the power to detoxify the body of years of toxins and to heal illnesses. Water fasting also has the virtue of helping you make a connection to Source.

Water fasting is a stand-alone treatment. It induces a powerful natural effect. This process allows the body to eliminate excess sodium and water from your body. Believe it or not, this process will resolve chronic problems with edema and will assist in reducing high blood pressure.

Water fasting offers extraordinary benefits for health and healing. There are studies that say it is the most effective treatment available for many conditions, as well as for diagnoses of life-threatening diseases.

Most water fasts last 24 to 72 hours. You should not follow a water fast for any longer than this without medical supervision.

Here are a few reasons why people try water fasting:
- Religious or spiritual reasons
- To lose weight
- To detoxify
- For health benefits
- Preparing for a medical procedure

The main reason people try water fasting is to improve their health.

Think about water fasting as a way to cleanse the body and get connected to Source before journeying with the Plant Spirit Medicine at a San Pedro or Ayahuasca ceremony. Again, please consult with a physician before attempting this type of fasting.

WHAT TO AVOID

Now is the time to pay attention to the DONT'S in regards to your dietary preparations. Now that we know the importance of the diet is to achieve the best benefits of the Plant Spirit Medicine, we should be eating fresh and healthy foods and drinking lots of water.

Just remember that what we will be giving up in food and drink is a sacrifice to the plant spirit and an acknowledgement of our respect for the process. We should feel that we are working as a team with the Plant Spirit Medicine.

Consult with your physician if you are taking any medications or have any medical conditions that would prevent you from attending a San Pedro or Ayahuasca ceremony or preparing for one.

We should avoid the following:
- Excessive sweets or desserts
- Fats and oils
- Alcohol
- Caffeine
- Recreational drugs (including marijuana)
- Sexual activity (It is not beneficial to release sexually, so you can keep your vital energy available for use in the healing process. Remember, you will be working with the medicine for over 12 hours in San Pedro and 5 to 6 in Ayahuasca.)

- No meat that is not fresh, smoked, canned or pickled

- No spices, such as salt, sugar or fake flavorings
- Limit citrus fruits and juices
- Processed foods and canned/packaged products
- Avoid plant based supplements
- Over ripe avocados/fruits to avoid spoiling or fermentation of the digestive tract
- Dairy that is aged or unfresh
- Coconut is ok as well as nut cheeses

Avoid the following in large quantities: (Due to their Tyramine content.) Tyramine is derived from the amino acid, Tyrosine. Blood pressure related problems can result from ingestion of large amount of tyramine-rich foods.

- Peanuts
- Raspberries
- Spinach
- Chocolate
- Tofu
- Miso
- Soybean paste
- Soy sauce
- Kimchi
- Pork and pork products

It is ok to consume:
- White meat chicken
- Eggs
- Fish

If you were thinking about becoming a vegetarian, this would be an excellent time to try it.

   Optional: I would recommend the following regimen for the ultimate preparation:
- Gluten/flour-free
- Sugar-free

- Quitting caffeine (or getting down to 1 cup a day)
- Taking probiotics
- Sleeping when the sun sets and waking up when the sun rises
- Experimenting with intermittent fasting

I suggest a light dinner, followed by only water and herbal tea until you drink at the ceremony the following morning.

MEDICATIONS AND HEALTH ISSUES

Every medication we take has its benefits, as well as possible side-effects, and San Pedro and Ayahuasca Plant Spirit Medicine is no exception.

When we talk about San Pedro Medicine, we have to mention that its common side-effect is increasing blood flow and heart rate. Remember, it is a heart medicine, after all, so, if you have a heart condition, you must talk to your Shaman or Physician about how to take the medicine. If you have a blood condition, you must be careful, as well. You may still be able to take the medicine but at a lower dosage.

Should I stop my medications before a San Pedro or Ayahuasca ceremony?

Again, you should consult with your doctor before stopping any medication since it is not smart to stop taking medicine 'cold turkey.' Many medications must be decreased in dosage before you stop taking it altogether.

Some medications should not be stopped at all, such as ones for diabetes, heart, blood pressure or any other condition that your health depends upon.

So, please talk to your doctor and see if you need to taper off for awhile. Only your doctor can advise you on how to best do this.

Other medicines that need to be addressed are anti-depressants that interact with the serotonin system. This should also include herbal medicine, anti-anxiety medicine, and recreational drugs such as cocaine, amphetamines, or ecstasy.

The following items should be stopped for at least one week prior to the ceremony:
- Cannabis/Marijuana
- Alcohol
- Cold/Cough Medicine
- Decongestants
- Sleeping Pills
- Sedatives
- Tranquilizers (Melatonin is accepted, your own body makes it)
- Diet Pills and Appetite Suppressants
- Allergy Medicine
- Barbiturates
- Opiates
- Antihistamines
- Some Hypertensive and Anti-hypertensive Medications

Remember that we prepare ourselves for San Pedro and Ayahuasca medicine in order to bring our bodies to its natural state. Even the following herbs must be avoided: Kava, Kratom, Ephedra, Ginseng, Yohimbe, Rhodiola Rosea, Kanna, Boswellia, Nutmeg, Scotch Broom, and Licorice Root.

ALTERNATIVE AND WESTERN MEDICINE
Before we get into a debate on Alternative and Complementary Medicine, let's determine exactly what we are talking about. Complementary and Alternative Medicine, also called CAM, is

the term for medical products and practices that are not part of standard medical care. Alternative Medicine includes such practices as massage, acupuncture, tai chi and even drinking green tea. Other examples are Chinese Medicine, Homeopathy, Naturopathy, and all natural health products such as herbs, supplements and probiotics. I am sure that you are currently using some of these alternative methods in your daily routine.

When I was young, my parents introduced me to Alternative Medicine such as homeopathic medication among others. It was part of their belief, and they shared it with my sister and me. The holistic or natural approach was part of my parent's philosophy.

My parents were fortunate to meet a very special person, Dr. Ricardo Alvarez, who specialized in homeopathic medicine. Throughout the years, my parents became very good friends with him and his family. I remember very interesting conversations between Dr. Alvarez and my parents. I didn't understand everything, but I did learn a lot from him that I still carry with me to this day. Dr. Alvarez went on to receive the title of President of Argentinean Homeopathic Association. I was grateful to know him.

My mother is a nurse, and she and my father are still using homeopathic medicine well into their 80's.

As a Healthcare Professional and Geriatric Specialist, I understand the importance of believing in Western Medicine for many diseases and illnesses, but I also believe in the benefits of Alternative Medicine as well. They can be a compliment to each other.

I strongly believe that we came into this world in a physical body to keep learning and evolving from previous experiences or lives. It's important to see ourselves in a holistic manner, while we take into consideration all the factors that can affect a human being on his or her current journey. This will not involve current or present issues, just issues that could have happened in the past, such as past lives, karma and ancestors.

All these factors will contribute to the person you were and help you understand the person you are today. Having this information can help you on your current path. It is up to you to select and determine which direction you want to follow.

Also included in complementary and alternative medicine is Akashic Records Readings, Angel Therapy, Past Life Regressions, Chakra Balancing and Alignment, just to name a few more modalities.

Being in a physical body in this century, Western Medicine is the one that governs our society. Western Medicine is a big business and very controlling. It is a major power of our economy.

However, in my personal experience, I believe that we need to select what feels right for us. We should align ourselves to what resonates and vibrates with our beliefs and needs. Being introduced to alternative medicine at such a young age, I have always felt that both medicines could complement each other. I felt this even stronger after my academic training and practice with western medicine for over 25 years.

I am not a physician, so I will not say which is more effective from a clinical point of view. Working with Alzheimer's patients and related dementias, I can honestly say that, many alternative methodologies are as effective as Western Medicine in many cases. Western Medicine is sometimes needed to achieve a fast result such as an antibiotic, but the complementation of both medicines is the best option.

I also believe that a medicine will be effective if you truly believe in the medicine that you are taking. Your belief, desire, and intention, along with your faith, will be converted into energy, and that conscious energy will be projected into the universe to achieve results. You must believe and trust the medicine that you incorporate into your lifestyle, so you can manifest the desired outcome.

When you select alternative or a more natural herb or plant medicine, the results could take a longer healing process. This is important to mention, as you need to prepare your body and your expectations toward the medicine that you are taking.

When you take Plant Spirit Medicine, you do it because you believe in it. The medicine, itself, will guide you to work on those areas that you need to work on, based on your intention and your communication with the Shaman, or whoever is in charge of the ceremony.

We take these Alternative Medicines because we believe in them and we prepare ourselves to take them as part of the treatment. It's all about believing, respecting and honoring ourselves and the medicines.

Whatever medicine you choose to take, make sure that you understand and research the pros and cons. Make sure you prepare yourself, so that you will receive the best benefit from whatever medicine you choose.

MENTAL HEALTH

The Plant Spirit Medicine can worsen such conditions as Schizophrenia and Psychosis. If you want to treat these issues, you should talk to a Physician since Plant Spirit Medicine will not help you.

Plant Spirit Medicine will help you with depression, bi-polar, and anxiety conditions. I must continue to stress how important it is to see a Physician or Shaman regarding your health concerns and conditions. The idea of all this is to help you and not harm you. We are doing all of the preparation in order for you to have a positive healing experience.

Do not underestimate your clinical or mental health status. This is why I am a firm believer in Complementary and Alternative Medicine with a Clinical Mind. In some cases, we can use Alternative Medicine instead of Western Medicine, but in other cases, we need to use them together so we can experience the best of both worlds and be safe.

If you are pregnant or lactating, you should not take the plant medicine. If you are not sure if you are pregnant, please wait until you know for sure.

I would also like to mention that some people have experienced miraculous healing with San Pedro and Ayahuasca Plant Spirit Medicine. Believe that you will experience a healing miracle.

CHAPTER 9: SPIRITUAL PREPARATION & SHAMANISM

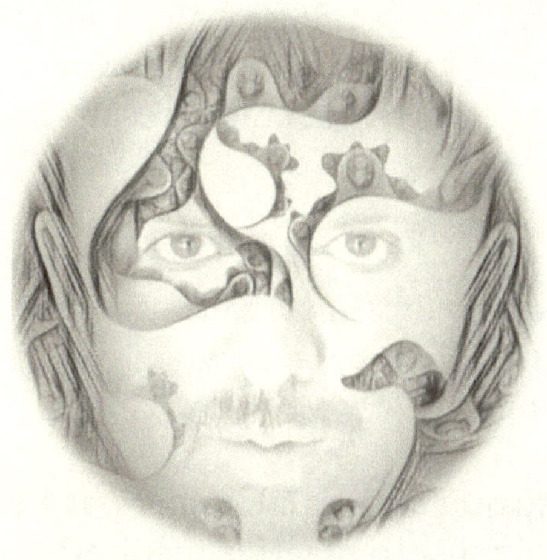

Breathe, close your eyes, relax and let things flow....
Since this is the only way that the universe works.... Humberto

PREPARING YOUR SPIRIT

When preparing spiritually for a Plant Spirit Medicine ceremony, choose what works for you. It may be praying, meditation, yoga, art or dance. As a musician, I connect myself with Source through singing songs that align my mind and soul. Along with this, guided meditation helps support and lead me to getting a deeper understanding of what I truly wish to accomplish at the ceremony.

Many times people go to a Plant Spirit Medicine ceremony thinking that they know what their intention is. Believe it or not, once you begin meditating on that subject, you may realize that your intention is a bit superficial. This is a perfect time to evaluate your intention and see if it is truly aligned

117

with your spirituality. Try to discover what type of spiritual method really works for you. Embrace the idea of going into a ceremony ready, prepared and spiritually connected with your desires, intention and the spirit of the plant. If you have already done a ceremony, you will understand how important it is to be aligned with the Plant Spirit Medicine and your goals.

Be disciplined and set specific times for your spiritual exercise, and remember that you can connect to Source whenever you like. With practice, you will see many results from this exercise.

MEDITATION

When it comes to meditation, I can only say that you must find the right time, the right type, and the right length of meditation that works for you.

I was not able to quiet my mind when I was alone. I tried many times at the beginning to practice meditation, and it just was not easy for me. As a matter of fact, it was very challenging and frustrating not to be able to follow everyone else in the room in a quiet manner, without my mind wandering all over the place.

This practice of meditation is to be able to reach mental clarity and a state of calm and emotional stability. It is important that you practice and feel comfortable in order to benefit from the process.

Personally, I found out that I needed guidance. I needed someone to lead me, manage my wandering mind, and help me relax. I began to understand and discover what would work for me. I found that guided meditation, mantras and Nydra Yoga worked perfectly. Now, I am even able to fall asleep, at times.

One of the benefits of falling asleep during a guided meditation is that your subconscious may still be listening. You can still be receiving the benefits. Nevertheless, the idea is for you to reach the meditative state while remaining conscious, in order to receive a more effective result.

Clinically, during meditation you are utilizing a part of your brain that processes things that the brain collects from your senses, such as taste, sight, smell, hearing and touch. You are using that part of the brain that gives you information about the world around you.

There are six popular types of meditation practices:
- Mindfulness Meditation
- Spiritual Meditation
- Focused Meditation
- Movement Meditation
- Mantra Meditation
- Transcendental Meditation

To be aligned with yourself and with Source, while you continue developing your spiritual strength, you should meditate two or three times a day. My personal suggestion is to implement it in your daily routine, especially in the morning and at night. Remember that you need to implement systems consciously. These meditations will become more than just a preparation for a ceremony. They will become your lifestyle and daily routine, to connect you with Source.

While I am meditating, I connect with my guides and my angels, as well. I suggest that you create a routine that resonates with you, your beliefs, and your intention. While meditating, allow your guides and angels to come to you. While communicating with them, your spirit will strengthen and be illuminated.

While I meditate, I concentrate on the positive and focus on abundance, praying that healing will remain in me and surround me.

Use meditation, praying, and yoga practices to help you reach that state of peace and balance as part of your preparation process for the Plant Spirit Medicine ceremony. Avoid all negative thoughts and negative people during this time. Don't watch any violent movies, so that you will be able to maintain that serene state you are looking for. Try to do this at least once a week, prior to the ceremony, so you will free yourself from negative energy. Keep in mind that the only thing that will promote negativity is fear and anxiety.

EXERCISE & PHYSICAL ACTIVITY
When you select the type of exercise that is good for you, you will know it by how it feels. Does it feel good? Is it enjoyable? Or is it just another job you have to do?

When you choose your exercise, it is recommended that you do it at least two weeks prior to attending a ceremony and hopefully, you'll continue to make it part of your daily routine after that.

Believe it or not, exercising is another important form of self-love.

Being fit for the ceremony is important, not just for the hormones exercise releases and the effect it has on your mental health, but the ceremony can be physically demanding on the body.

Since the ceremony is usually done during the daytime, the connection to nature is a blessing and a major element of the healing that the medicine provides. Go for a daily walk or touch the earth in a calming and natural setting to begin connecting to the plant spirit.

Personally, I use the physical preparation to connect with Source through my body and mind. Being physically ready for a ceremony helped me enjoy all of the activities and rituals. I have seen others rolling all over the floor and even jumping up and down, so being fit can help you greatly.

As part of the physical aspect, abstaining from sexual activity is important as well. When you experience physical contact or sexual activity with other people, you absorb their energies, and these energies are stored at all levels of your being. The idea is to focus on cleansing and balancing YOUR energies so you can bring them to a natural state. You need to concentrate on harmonizing your own energies. Try to limit your interaction with large crowds. Concentrate on your balance and avoid bars, concerts, and clubs.

Part of your physical preparation can be just sitting by yourself in silence. The benefits of this cannot be overstated. I recommend that you do this for between 10 minutes to an hour a day. You will find that you begin listening to your intuitive knowledge, and that will help you in the healing process. This exercise will assist you in developing the capacity to comprehend and integrate messages.

I am not an expert on exercising, so I won't tell you which type of exercise you should choose, but I will make some suggestions. Walking, jogging, running, dancing and/or aerobics are a few that I am familiar with. Any type of exercise is good as long as you are moving your body in a daily or weekly routine. Once you begin this routine, you will experience many benefits. Exercise will detoxify harmful chemicals from your body which is what you want to do before you attend a Plant Spirit Medicine ceremony. You want to be clean and in as natural a state as possible.

Exercise will also help you to alleviate symptoms of depression that you may have, as well as protecting your brain. Researchers say that physical activity can help to eliminate a substance from your blood that accumulates during stressful moments and which can impact the function of the brain negatively.

Exercise offers a lot of benefits to your body beyond just the physical and it's free! Hormones, such as adrenaline and cortisol can assist in alleviating stress and depression. Adrenaline is also called epinephrine. It is a hormone that your body makes in times of crisis or while exercising. Adrenaline can make your heart beat faster and work harder while you exercise. This process will increase your blood flow to your muscles and make you more alert. In a way, adrenaline is a messenger in your brain. Adrenaline will also maximize blood glucose levels primarily for the brain. It will redistribute blood to the muscles and alter the body's metabolism.

Cortisol creates a surge of energy, focus, and motivation while exercising. That's why people say, "Go and take a walk and get your thoughts straight." It's a way of relaxing and refocusing. I'm sure you have done this many times.
If you think that exercise doesn't provide you with more than just a toned body, you are so wrong!

Did you know that exercising also stimulates the production of endorphins? Well, it does. This chemical, produced by the body, works as a natural pain killer and mood elevator, as well as a stress reliever. It works like a drug that helps you relieve pain because the endorphins interact with your brain, reducing the perception of pain. Endorphins are only one of the many transmitters released when you exercise.

Physical activity also stimulates the release of dopamine, norepinephrine and serotonin. Dopamine is known as the 'feel good' neurotransmitter. It is a chemical that transports information among the neurons, and it controls and regulates your mood. Dopamine is released when you are engaging in sexual activity, eating a delicious meal or doing something that gives you pleasure. Serotonin helps to regulate your mood. When you have low levels of Serotonin, you may be diagnosed with depression and also experience decreased sexual arousal.

SELF-DISCOVERY

You must take the time to discover yourself and initiate your communication with the spirit of the plant. This is how you will learn about the medicine that you will be taking and how it is worked by the Coordinator or Shaman. Self-discovery is very important so you can be in touch with your fears and emotions while confronting them in a ceremony.

Through hidden emotions from past traumas that you have been suppressing, will come knowledge and wisdom, by facing them when you attend a Plant Spirit Ceremony. If you work consciously, discovering yourself, you will understand that most of these issues and traumas come from childhood. The spirit of the plant will take you to those memories. These are memories that you carry over into your adult life and are revealed in how you handle stress, depression, anxiety and how you connect to others. At the ceremony, you will be healing your inner child, while working with your shadows, emotional pain, and discomfort.

Participating in a Plant Spirit Ceremony requires trust, faith and confidence in yourself, as well as in the healing medicine. You should work on this during your spiritual preparation. Be responsible and honest with your feelings. Another important question you should ask yourself is, whether you are willing to embody this process as a spiritual discipline.

I used the process to align myself with the willingness to surrender to letting go of the parts that no longer serve me. This is a perfect time to concentrate on exercising compassion, gratitude, love and acceptance toward yourself and others. I always say that gratitude is the basis of any healing process. Try not to be hard on yourself while confronting these uncomfortable memories, and concentrate on the healing transformation.

Taking time to prepare your mental and spiritual body, in addition to your physical one, is your goal. Being able to connect with yourself will assist you when you write your intention. Many individuals often realize that their intentions are a bit superficial, and what they really need to work on lies more on the spiritual level. Plant Spirit Medicines work with your subconscious mind and will help you see what truly matters.

HOW TO RAISE YOUR VIBRATION

Understanding the importance of 'raising your vibration' will help you in the preparation, as you will be able to increase your level of energy, your happiness, your health and your overall success.

When you are feeling good, it seems like you have an overabundance of energy. That is just 'you' having a 'high vibration.' It is a feeling that once you have experienced it, you will want to work on it every day. You'll feel like smiling and taking on the world!

You will also know for sure when your vibration is low. You will resonate to a low vibration if you are sad, angry, jealous, or have any other negative emotion. That lower emotion will lower your vibration, making you feel tired and unmotivated. You can get sick from this if you don't raise your vibration.

Raising your vibration will be nothing but beneficial. When you raise your vibration, you will start to see drastic positive changes in your life, as well as boosting your immune system.

If you are knowledgeable about the Law of Attraction, you will know that good things seem to happen when you are uplifted. The Law of Attraction will work for you if you are feeling good.

Your vibration will be raised, and you will be attracting the things you want in your life. You will need to desire and visualize what you want, and that will raise your vibration! Without raising your vibration, you can't get yourself on the same frequency as the things you want to attract.

The following is a list of ways that you can raise your vibration:

Start by being more appreciative and grateful. You can begin with friends and family. Be appreciative of the food you have to eat and anything else you may have. The key is to really mean it. You can also start a ritual by writing down a list of great things that are happening in your life. Making these small changes a daily habit will make you feel good, and your vibration will be higher than ever.

Question yourself on how aware you are of your current vibration. How much time do you spend on gossip or complaining in general? Remember that your thoughts and words are very powerful, and if you are always thinking negative thoughts, your frequency will lower and you will attract negative things to your life.

Listen to and enjoy music. It will help you raise your vibration and trigger positive emotions. Listen to positive music with positive lyrics that will help you focus your thoughts on positive perspectives.

Exercise and meditate. Exercise releases endorphins while triggering positive feelings. It helps to give you a positive outlook on life. Meditation will help to relieve stress and clear your mind, so you can focus on things that are truly important.

Practice Yoga, Reiki or Chi for balancing your energy.

You can also listen to an audio file 528 hz. This is known as the 'love frequency' channel. It is truly remarkable how much better you will feel after playing 528 hz for awhile.

- Focus on positivity. Surround yourself with positive people.
- Eat healthy foods.
- Practice forgiveness.
- Take a nice, warm bath or a long hot shower.
- Do things that you love! Don't waste your time doing things that you don't enjoy.
- Take a nap. Sometimes you feel a bit down just because you're tired.

SHAMAN HISTORY

Shamanism is especially associated with the Native People of Siberia in Northern Asia, where Shamanic practices have been noted for centuries by Asian and Western visitors. It is an ideology that used to be widely practiced in Europe, Asia, Tibet, North and South America and Africa.

Currently, we see many communities in different areas of the world getting more involved in researching diverse Shaman traditions.

Shamanism believes the causes of disease lie in the spiritual realm, inspired by malicious spirits. Many Shamans are experts in working with Plant Spirit Medicines or native plants and herbs from their area of the world. They prescribe these medicines and herbs to their patients. The Shaman will work with the spirit of the plant while learning its effects and healing properties from them.

Remember that all Shamans have their own lineage and traditions that they follow. The Shamans and Curanderos from the Peruvian Amazon Basin use medicine songs called 'Icaros' to evoke spirits. The interesting thing concerning 'song medicine' is that they will sing songs that they will learn from their guides. Many times, they will go into a trance and sing songs that they are channeling from the other side during the treatment and ceremony.

Shamans will also use 'Totemic' items, such as rocks with special powers. An animated spirit in the Shaman is common to observe as well.

These practices are very ancient. In Latin America, the use of witchcraft and sorcery, known as 'brujeria' still exist in certain societies.

Those with Shamanic knowledge usually enjoy great power and prestige in the community. On the other hand, they can also be regarded suspiciously or fearfully, as potentially harmful to others.

As a professional singer and performer, I would like to mention the role that music plays in my life and how it became my true religion. Music was and is a part of my connection with Source. Ever since I can remember, I felt I could connect with other dimensions through music. The music I used for my first production, 'TANGObsession' came to me in less than a day in a list that I began creating while lying in my bed. I only wrote the names of the songs. I would use, and then how to create a story from those songs. The interesting part of this process was to see the final result. The sequence in which the songs were presented to me by my guides originally became the order in which they were performed and also formed the story line of the show. This unique creation was full of vibrations that I was able to feel while being on stage as the main character. This vibration was visual to me in that I could literally see the aura/energy of my audience.

I was in a state of connecting and surrendering to Source when all of this just came to me. I am in the process of creating a new show; 'Madame Yvonne' and the process is happening again. This process of allowing requires practice, studying and surrendering so you can hear the voices of your guides as they communicate with you. I shared this process with very few people, and fewer still really understood about the impact this had on me and what a beautiful experience it was.

I can say that there are times when I can transport myself to a different dimension and be able to create melodies or lyrics without even thinking about them. In a way, it's happening to me as I create this book, as well. In many chapters, I can be clinical and rational and in others, more connected with the guides as they help me to give you messages.

I also want to mention that we all have the ability to connect and channel other entities and vibrations. We need to find the way to do this and keep practicing, so it will come to us in a more organic and easier way. Shamans are able to do it very naturally and quickly because of their connections, and they practice daily, as well. If you consciously practice, I am sure you will be able to experience this one day.

THE PURPOSE OF A SHAMAN
Purpose, Role and Shamanism

It is important to understand the purpose and role of a Shaman. Throughout the book, I refer to a Facilitator, Shaman or Coordinator. The difference is the type of experience that each one has with the Plant Spirit Medicine or methodology.

I am showing respect to the Shamans in this section of the book and honoring them for their work and their beliefs.

A Shaman is a person who will access or work with the world of 'good and evil spirits.' This definition is usually related to the people of Northern Asia and North America, who enter into a trance-like state during a ritual or methodology such as divination and/or healing.

The word, Shaman comes from the Siberian Tungusic word for

the person in a tribe of indigenous people who uses a type of magic to heal or foresee future events; someone who communicates with spirits, plants, animals and other worlds.

The following statement is not a sexist one, but Shamans are usually men that are also called 'Medicine Men' or 'Curanderos.' They can also be called 'Witch Doctor' or 'Vegetalistas,' among other names.

Two fantastic Shamans were put in my path when my interest and need for an energy healing treatment began. The two females came to me in different ways. One of them came to a class that I was teaching on voice lessons. She was originally from Tucumán, Argentina and I knew her through a mutual friend. Machi is a very clever and talented Shaman. She always told me to 'let my duendes free' (goblins). The other Shaman came to my Art Studio for Theater and Psychodrama classes a few years ago. She not only became a student, but also my teacher and initiator in the art of healing. She is originally from Bolivia and had a father from my country of Argentina. I had amazing experiences with her teachings and ceremonies.

It is important to pay attention and welcome these special individuals when they come into your life.

We can say that Shamanism is a religious practice that involves a Practitioner; a Shaman who is believed to interact with the spirit world through altered states of consciousness, such as a trance.

Shamans are chosen by other generations in traditional families, continuing a lineage or they receive a calling to their role. The ones that are chosen by their families are chosen because of their knowledge, spiritual gifts, sensibility, relationships to other Shamans, or they have something else unique about them.

Believe it or not, many Shamans are reluctant to accept the role at the beginning. This is because of the physical aspect and duties, and what they demand. The truth is that if a person's purpose is to become a Shaman, the spirit world will not let that person rest until he accepts.

The Shaman's job is to journey into the spirit world or non-ordinary reality, getting advice and powers to maintain the balance between the natural and the supernatural. (Harner, 1982). The Shamans will use many techniques and methods during their journey by altering their consciousness through ritual methods, such as drumming, dancing, chanting and/or the use of psychotropic plants. In some cases, Indian Shamans will use chants and Plant Spirit Medicine to achieve their altered state.

There are many variations and forms of Shamanism throughout the world, but several common beliefs are shared by all forms of Shamanism. Common beliefs identified by Eliade (1972) are:

• Spirits exist and they play important roles, both in human lives and in human society.

• The Shaman can communicate with the spirit world.

• Spirits can be benevolent and malevolent.

• The Shaman can treat sickness caused by malevolent spirits.
• The Shaman can employ trances, including techniques to incite visionary ecstasy and go on vision quests.

• The Shaman's spirit can leave the body to enter the supernatural world to search for answers.

• The Shaman evokes animal images as spirit guides, omens and message bearers.

• The Shaman can perform other varied forms of divination, using objects such as crystal balls, throwing bones, runes reading, and sometimes, foretelling of future events.

SOUL & SPIRIT CONCEPTS

I would like to talk a little about the Shaman's beliefs, so we can begin to understand their practices. Shamans believe in Soul Dualism or multiple souls. This is a system of beliefs in which a person has two or more souls. In many cases, one of the souls is associated with body functions ('free soul' or 'wandering soul').

The 'free soul' is said to leave the body and journey to the spirit world during sleep, a trance-like state, delirium, insanity, and death. Soul Dualism is also seen by certain cultures as a 'soul loss' or an illness and to be healed. You must return to the 'free soul' which may have been stolen by an evil spirit or got lost in the spirit world. It is relevant to mention that this belief is also seen as a healing practice.

If healing is the process of the restoration of health from an unbalanced, diseased, or damaged organism, people that believe in Shamanism and the power of Shamans will be seeking them for healing purposes. Many cultures believe that the role of a Shaman consists of the supposed retrieval of the lost soul of the ill person. The culture will determine how many souls a person should have. Some cultures believe that a person may have more than six souls. Spirits are invisible entities that only Shamans can see, and some of these spirits are in physical form. They are seen as persons that can assume a human or animal body. Some animals, in their physical forms, are also seen as spirits such as in the case of the eagle, snake, jaguar and rat.

Another practice performed by Shamans is the Ecstatic Dance. It is a form of dance in which the dancers do not feel the need to follow specific steps, and they abandon themselves to the rhythm. They move freely as the music takes them, leading to a trance and a feeling of ecstasy. Ecstatic Dance has been practiced throughout human history and is still practiced today. Rhythmic drumming is used to alter consciousness in spiritual practices, as well.

Along with Icaros; medicine songs, is an essential part of the rituals and ceremonies. Drums are also used by Shamans. The beating of the drum allows the Shaman to achieve an altered state of consciousness, while he travels on a journey between the spiritual and physical worlds. Much fascination surrounds the role of the acoustics the Shaman uses in a ceremony. Shaman drums are generally constructed from animal skin stretched over a bent, wooden hoop with a handle across the top.

'Vigils,' a period of intentional sleeplessness, is also part of the Shaman's beliefs and practices, as well as fasting for purification and cleansing.

In many Shamanic cultures, 'Sweat Lodges' are also part of their cleansing process. A sweat lodge is a simple hut, typically dome-shaped or oblong and made with natural materials. The structure is the lodge and the ceremony performed within the structure is called a 'purification ceremony.'

Remember that Shamans may use varying materials in spiritual practice based on their lineage, culture and traditions.

Personally, I truly believe that when you learn the lyrics of a song and you perform it, you will be aligned or in contact with the spirits. I can attest to that. Many times, I have felt emotions on how to perform a certain song in a specific way without having any previous knowledge about how to do it. It is very personal, and everyone will have their own experience. I can say that when I sing songs today, I receive unconscious advice on how to perform and manage my voice with certain tones and character.

SHAMAN ROLE

Shamans perform a variety of functions and activities, depending on their respective cultures, lineage, and traditions, as I have mentioned before. They perform healing, lead sacrifices, preserve traditions, perform storytelling, sing songs, tell fortunes, and act as 'guides of souls.' A single Shaman may perform several of these functions. In some ceremonies, you will have a Shaman and an assistant or more than one Shaman. Together, they will work as a team in rituals and diverse steps of the ceremony, under the leadership of a Shaman or a Coordinator established by the group.

Remember that the fundamental understanding of anyone committing to a Shamanic path is that there are good and bad energies (spirits) all around us, and a Shaman aids in protection and clearing.

I am usually very cautious about attending a ceremony. I have had good experiences but I have heard, first hand, about cases that got out of hand, and the outcome and the experience of the Shaman were questionable.

Whoever knows me, knows that I do not seek out information; information comes to me. I always wondered why. When information comes to me I process it and use it to help others. This is one of those cases. Having the information doesn't mean that I have to be explicit on what I was told, as I did not experience it myself.

Please understand the importance of the Shaman's role in a ceremony. It is crucial that you know who you will be working with and meet with them prior to the ceremony.

The Shaman is the 'bridge walker' traveling to other realms

to help with soul retrieval and spiritual cleansings that impact the tangible (body) and the intangible such as the soul, mind, emotions.

Shamans face many sacrifices along their path. They dedicate their lives and will sacrifice every last attachment and move through every conceivable fear. Being a Shaman is not a job, it's one's whole life. To most people, being a Shaman is a blessing, but not to some individuals. In most cases, the Shaman surrenders to their mission and path.

One of the nice things I have learned through my research and from many Shamans is how to understand suffering and not eradicate it. This last statement is what makes me more able to comprehend the relationship between western traditional medicine and alternative and complementary medicine.

A Lightworker once called me an Alchemist due to my way of thinking and how I view medicine from a very holistic and organic manner. However, I don't think that I want any title or degree to determine who I am. I have enough degrees, certificates and diplomas from my birth country and my adopted one, and I am still learning and evolving, like everyone else. I am just a messenger and a bridge of knowledge enjoying the fact that I can share with others like I am doing at this precise moment with you.

Going back to the role of Shaman, I would like to say that the Shaman becomes a vessel of divinity. The Shaman will become a person of love and a guide who will be communicating with the Plant Spirit Medicine. He/She will be guiding you and others.

Sometimes the Shaman will help you understand your true essence while working with other entities for your healing. They can help you understand your eternal nature and help you become aware that everything is both real and not real; that we are both mortal and immortal.

Aside from all of the work the Shaman does, he/she will still be protecting you while you are in the ceremony. Since you are going to be under the effect of the medicine, the Shaman will be protecting you from low energies that can interfere with your state of mind.

Now that you know everything that the Shaman will be doing; leading the ceremony, giving you the medicine, curing or treating you, cleansing you and protecting you from low energies so you can work with the plant spirit medicine, my question is….would you like to know who the Shaman leading your ceremony is?

Make sure that you work with an authentic Shaman or a knowledgeable and experienced Coordinator.

SHAMAN COACHING

Making a list of some personal information about yourself will assist your Coordinator in understanding what treatments or rituals you should attend during the Plant Spirit Medicine ceremony. Not every person who conducts a ceremony will request this information. The more that the Coordinator knows about your intention and your history, the better it will be for your healing process. While generating this list, make sure you do it honestly and simply.

Begin the list with:

•   Your full name and date of birth

•   Describe yourself in a few words. Include your values, fears and any gifts that you may possess.

• Describe your childhood and list memories from it. Be very honest here. If you are describing a painful memory from your past, describe it in detail. Describe happy moments as well as not so happy ones.

Go for it and begin the stage of confronting and working with your fears and possible traumas that you thought you were over but are still in your mind.

As part of your journey, you have probably encountered people transitioning to the other side. How did you feel about that? Was it a relevant person in your life? Take the time to include as many as you remember in your narrative.

On a more personal level, try to write about those people that you love the most and those that caused you pain. You will also want to share if you are divorced or having problems letting go. This is important for the Shaman or Coordinator to know because it usually involves a 'cutting energetic cords' ritual in the ceremony. Make sure you have the full birth name of the person you want to name in the cutting cords or spiritual divorce ritual in order for it to be effective.

Some Shamans or Coordinators perform a special ritual for women that have experienced a miscarriage or womb problems. This is another reason to prepare yourself and write your narrative.

It is not expected for you to write a book about your life, but it is important to be direct and to the point about your issues. Be honest with your descriptions.

Having a narrative will help you organize and identify issues that you will want to work on during the ceremony. It is a great working tool for the Coordinator as well.

Remember that Plant Spirit Medicine healing begins from the time you decide to be part of the ceremony. From that moment, your commitment and search begins with a journey filled with self-love and abundance.

CHAPTER 10: CEREMONY

Being you is easy when you put your soul, mind and spirit in one aligned vibration....where love and harmony is your vortex without limits....HF

A ceremony is a unified, ritualistic event with a purpose, usually consisting of a number of artistic components performed on a special occasion. The word may be of Etruscan origin, via the Latin caerimonia (Wikipedia). It is a formal act or ritual that is usually prepared or performed in observation of a specific intention that could be based on a rite or a series of rites.

The purpose of a ceremony is to allow us to acknowledge a transition or a rite of passage with a belief and specific intention, that could be a new beginning or sometimes, a conclusion.

Understanding terminology or taking the time to define a word can really help us assimilate and accept something in a rational manner.

For some of us, when we rationalize, a certain process will

allow us to assimilate things organically at a rapid pace. It can happen so fast that we don't even notice when the process has ended.

It is important to take the time to understand yourself and honor the process. There is no right or wrong. There is only 'what works for you.'

Therefore, if you need to determine what a ceremony is, I would say it is the opportunity to dive into yourself and become honest and truthful with your feelings, while remembering who you are, in a profound way.

When we participate in a ceremony, we understand that it will be something sacred and/or a matter of transition or transformation of some sort. We will be honoring the Spirit of the Plant that will be leading us to the healing that we are searching for.

A ceremony will offer you a powerful method for healing, personal transformation and growth where you will be able to be in touch with your inner self, while receiving messages and much needed information.

Whenever I have attended a ceremony, I have experienced some of the most amazing and potent experiences of my lifetime. They have allowed me to see, understand, and integrate information that I was hungry for as part of my evolvement and growth.

The integration of this information in the last part of the ceremony gave me so much wisdom to be processed on my journey.

CEREMONY COORDINATOR

This is a very important subject. I have heard so many horror stories and comments from different people who have had very different experiences with Coordinators.

Throughout this book, I have mentioned how much I believe

in preparing yourself for any ceremony. It is as important as participating physically. Part of the preparation is knowing your Coordinator or Facilitator. Finding out who will be guiding you in the ceremony is part of your preparation.

Not only will you know firsthand, who the person is, but you can also work on your personal coaching or set up a private meeting with your Coordinator, so he or she will know ahead of time, exactly what your intention is, and what you want to work on.

I have never had a bad experience, or any problems with any of the ceremonies that I have attended. As a healer, I can understand how many things could go wrong if you do the medicine with an inexperienced Coordinator. I suggest to everyone to do their due diligence. This is like selecting a physician or specialist for an ailment that you need healed. I will go even further and say that this is someone who will work with more than one body at a time and still guide you through a healing process.

Therefore, if you are going to put yourself into someone's hands to work with your physical, spiritual and emotional body, wouldn't you like to know everything about that person? Think about it.

I'm just going to continue on with what you have control over and assist you in preparing yourself to understand the role of the Coordinator.

CEREMONY PREPARATION

Ceremony preparation is crucial, in my opinion, and is the actual beginning of the ceremony itself. This preparation is not only important for you, but for the coordinator assisting you, as well.

After participating in many rituals and ceremonies and reading diverse material about them, I can fully understand the importance of the preparation routine.

The more we dive into it and practice energy work, we expand our consciousness with its power and benefits. It is a way of incorporating the work, not only rationally, but also spiritually, while we practice and experience the benefits and teachings. We will be able to talk about what we believe in and do it. This is why it is important to prepare oneself for a Plant Spirit Medicine ceremony.

I've been in ceremonies where the Coordinator was not 100% prepared, and you could feel the energy was all over the place. You could tell that the energy was not aligned with the intention, and the items used at the ceremony were not prepared to be used properly. Preparing should be taken very seriously and consciously by everyone.

For me, the ceremony begins from the time I commit myself to it and begin the process of honoring myself and the ceremony itself. It is like a communion of sorts. The personal ritual allows me to center myself and align my thoughts and intentions. Having this communion between San Pedro and myself was the beginning of my journey in discovering healing treatments.

There are occasions when you go to a ceremony or a ritual that is not 100% aligned with the energy you were expecting. You need to take responsibility for your own experience when this happens. If you are prepared and have a clear intention, you will benefit from the event regardless because you will be ready to work with the plant spirit and your intentions.

Usually the preparation for a ceremony will consist of: diet, meditations, exercise, and any other rituals that you may do already, as well as coaching work. You can elect to do coaching work prior to the ceremony by the coordinator or the Shaman.

The healthy daily routine is not just about diet and exercise, but about doing things that you enjoy and bring you pleasure. Take care of your emotional state as well as the spiritual and physical.

It is important to begin preparing yourself for a ceremony with a body cleansing at least 7 to 10 days before you go. This was introduced to me by my teacher (Shaman from Bolivia) as well as other Shamans and Nutritionists. They showed me the importance of this step from the clinical and physical point of view. One of the benefits from this preparation is that the Plant Spirit Medicine works better when our bodies are purified and aligned physically, emotionally and energetically with the natural cycle of nature.

If you did your research before going to a ceremony or ritual, you would understand how important it is to know your Coordinator before the event. I am used to having a conversation with a Coordinator prior to the event. This communication assists me in achieving my goals. The Coordinator will be guiding you throughout the ceremony and helping you to work on your intentions and issues.

The idea of having a meeting with the Coordinator was presented to me by a teacher for coaching purposes. The idea is to get a better outcome in an organized manner. The Coordinator can help you with your intentions in an organic and beautiful way.

If you narrow down your intentions, as I do, you will be able to work with the Coordinator on those intentions. It will also give you peace of mind because your conscious and subconscious will have this information pre-registered, and it will not be a surprise in the ceremony. Remember, you are in control, and you are attending this ceremony for your healing with a clear purpose.

The preparation with your Coordinator will be used as part of the work during the ceremony and will help you to better fulfill your purpose.

I would like to re-enforce the relevancy of the diet and herbs used for preparation

In order to have a full experience, I would recommend doing the cleansing for 10 days, as well as communicating with the Coordinator. This process should be taken seriously in order to have the full experience of the Plant Spirit Medicine.

After doing many preparations for ceremonies and rituals, I can understand how convents, cults and diverse groups have a daily routine as part of their intention and mission. I understand how relevant it is. It is so easy to get distracted on a daily basis, so a routine would be a good solution in helping us attain our goals.

In general, having a healthy, daily routine allows us to stay grounded. Following a routine helps us to be drama free while we cleanse our bodies. With herbs and diet, our bodies will be able to release toxins and stress, as well as all of the other things we do not need. I believe this is essential for a healthy, organic lifestyle.

YOU CAN DO IT!

THE MESA OR ALTAR
MAn Altar is also called a mesa and is usually portable or created at the ceremony location. It is used in Shamanic healing and Plant Spirit Medicine ceremonies. The purpose of the Altar is to connect with the natural world like a bridge.

The origin of the Mesa is in the Latin American countries. The word 'Mesa' is a Spanish term which means table, or a high plateau, or a place where the Shamans go to meet the spirits. It is a Shamanic Altar used for healing ceremonies and prayer.

Shamans and ceremony Coordinators use this Altar in their healing ceremonies and prayers to connect them with Source and to meet with the spirits and ancestors. Many more cultures around the world have used some sort of a Mesa or Altar.

Let's understand that a Mesa can be a permanent table or something as small or simple as a cloth and a few stones. It contains sacred tools such as stones, feathers and other sacred items that have been collected over the years by its owner. They are usually folded into a square and tied with a cloth band or Mesa tie. This helps to keep the tools safe and the Mesa portable.

CEREMONY PROCESS

Each Coordinator will lead a San Pedro ceremony differently. That is why I suggest that you talk to the Coordinator prior to the ceremony. That way, you will know the steps and process before you go.

Because ceremonies can be performed in many ways, it does not mean that one way is correct and another isn't. There is no specific way to perform the ceremony. It's best to do your research before you go so you will be prepared. You don't want surprises because they can take you away from your concentration or your intent. That does not mean that the healing will not happen, but you don't want to waste time or energy trying to deal with something that you should have known prior to attending the ceremony.

When I go to a ceremony or ritual, I want to be as relaxed as possible. I want to be able to open myself up and be able to channel my Guides and Archangels. This is why I emphasize preparation.

Many ceremonies are performed all over the world and have been for centuries. Everyone does them based on their traditions, ancestors, teachers, lineage and, the personal gifts that they may possess.

A Plant Spirit Medicine ceremony has many rituals or steps that you may go through. You will experience an introduction where all participants introduce themselves and verbalize their intention for the ceremony. This is a great way to 'break the ice' and begin feeling comfortable with your peers. Remember, you will be spending over 10 hours with them.

It is custom and respectful, as part of the sacred ceremony, to ask permission of the Ancestors and the plant medicine to allow us to work with them and with their spirits. It is also normal to ask them to help us receive the messages from the Plant Spirit Medicine and its healing.

It is also very nice, when, at the beginning of the ceremony, you may experience the Salutation to the Four Directions.

THE EAST represents spring and symbolizes victory, success and power. Words are offered to the East so they may fly and soar with spirit.

THE NORTH represents the winter and also a sense of trouble, hardship and sadness. The animals representing the North include white buffalo, moose and bear, reminding us to be patient with the seasons.

THE WEST represents autumn and the final harvest at the end of a cycle. The West is black, and it represents the death of summer's cycle.

THE SOUTH represents summer and is a time of great abundance. The summer holds fertility, passion, growth, joy, and peace. The color is white. The animals of the South hold the lesson of strength, courage and pride; the eagle with her keen sight, and the wolf, proud to be part of the tribe.

While setting the intention of the ceremony, some 'smudging' will be performed to clear negative energies before you take the sacred medicine.

As I mentioned before, every Coordinator will perform their ceremony based on their lineage and traditions, but you may experience the following services:

(1) Protection Prayer, Tobacco Ceremony or an Offering (2) Chakra Balancing for good energy flow
(3) Cleansing. Don't be surprised to be part of group rituals during the ceremony.

You may also receive individual healing based on your pre-work done with the Coordinator. He or she will have you participate in a specific ritual like 'cutting cords or vows' or even a 'womb healing' for women.

Despacho or Ofrenda (offering), at the end of the ceremony will be performed by the Coordinator with everyone's participation. This is something my Teacher always does, and it's a moment in which we truly honor and give thanks to our ancestors, the Plant Spirit Medicine, and anyone involved in the ceremony who was contributing to the process.

The Healer will work with the spirits, singing, passing you codes and messages while cleansing and healing your body and spirit throughout the ceremony.

You should go with an open mind and be prepared, so you will know what to expect and be able to have a full healing experience at your Plant Spirit Medicine ceremony, working with yourself and your ancestors.

WHAT TO WEAR AND WHAT TO BRING

Be comfortable and prepare the things that you will need for the ceremony. I recommend that you ask the Coordinator or Shaman for a list of things that will be provided for you. Some places will provide you with blankets, pillows and lawn chairs. Remember that you will be at the ceremony for at least 10 or more hours, so dress very comfortably. Take into consideration the weather forecast of the day, so that you have everything you may need. You don't want to have anything break the concentration of your intention.

Here is a list of things you may need or want to bring:

Obviously, yourself....Be ready to discover yourself and work with the medicine openly, while surrendering and allowing the healing that the medicine has for you.

Make sure you have someone to pick you up after the ceremony. If not, have the UBER application in your phone, so you can request a ride back home. DO NOT DRIVE after taking the medication.
Clothing will be according to the temperature of the season. Make sure you bring extra clothing in case of rain during the ceremony or vomiting from a reaction to the medicine. In many cases, you need to release what no longer serves you. This may or may not happen to you.

Some other items you may want to bring are:

• Yoga mat, sleeping bag or something to sleep on (strongly recommended)
• A small container, in case you cannot get to the area assigned for vomiting. The Coordinator will let you know where that area is prior to the ceremony.

• If a blanket is not provided for you, I recommend that you bring one to cover yourself if needed to get warm.

• If a chair is not provided, bring a lawn chair, as the ceremony is outside and you will want to be comfortable. I bring a beach chair that reclines or a cushion or something to sit on.

• Sun protection and mosquito repellent, a hat, or scarf

• Stones, amulets, etc. to accompany you on your experience if you desire

• A notebook and a pen, or even a small computer to write any messages that you may receive and want to remember

• Fresh flowers for the Altar or MESA. Ask the Coordinator about this prior to the ceremony.

• Wear comfortable clothes.

• Alkaline or coconut water and fresh organic foods to be shared with the group at the end of the ceremony (fruit, nuts, bread, juice, hummus, etc.)

• Remember that it is not permitted to drink during the ceremony. Discuss this with your Coordinator prior to the ceremony.

• Women who are in their 'Moon Time' (Menstruation) should talk to the Shaman prior to the ceremony)

Participation is restricted for people who have recent fractures or surgeries, acute infectious diseases, epilepsy, and for anyone taking any type of drug (natural or synthetic). Talk to your Shaman for further explanation.

These medications should be discontinued at least 15 days prior to the ceremony: Anti-depressives, weight loss pills, anti-hypertensives, asthma and flu medicines, nervous disorder medication, among others.

In the case of psychiatric medicine, it is absolutely necessary to consult your physician.

Ayahuasca Ceremonies have many rules, so always consult with your Shaman or Coordinator for the specific steps that they want you to follow. Limit your water intake prior to the ceremony and do not drink during the ceremony, as it will dilute the effect of the medicine.

CHAPTER 11: AFTERMATH

When you think that love has betrayed
you...Think again.... Was it love?....
Or was it a lesson for you to learn?...HF

ASSIMILATING AND INTEGRATING

Assimilating and integrating is as important as what you learn from and during a Plant Spirit Medicine ceremony. We need to receive the information and then assimilate it and process it, so it remains with us as part of what we have learned.

Integration is a way of receiving information and allowing ourselves to be open to the messages as part of our evolution. After we receive the messages, what do we do with it? How do we incorporate those messages into our lifestyle?

In my case, I needed to rationalize it. It needed to make sense to me in order to assimilate it much easier, without resistance from my brain. I know my process will be easier if I begin with that first step. I will not resist the messages that come to me through emotions because the rationalization process doesn't begin until after the message is received. What I am trying to say is, you need to know yourself, accept yourself, and what works for you or what doesn't. This will make the process easier.

DISCOVER YOURSELF!

I know myself, and I need at least 24 hours to process change. I discovered this when I was working on myself regarding my happiness. I think it is important to take the time and understand how your thought processes work.

I am a great receptor. I am like a sponge. This could be good and not so good. I can observe and receive many types of information at once, but through the years, I realized that I needed more time for my brain and mind to process all the information coming to me. By taking more time, the assimilation process became easier and healthier for me; more organic. After I go through my thought processes, I will know right away if the information received makes sense and if it is aligned to my beliefs. If something doesn't feel natural, I will know it right away.

If there is something that does not align organically with you, now is the time to begin questioning and researching why it doesn't feel good. Getting to the bottom of why it doesn't align is taking conscious responsibility, and that is appropriate. You may have to confront some fears, but you need to get to the bottom of the situation.

Details are important to me because I like to learn and form an opinion about things. The opinion would be whether I feel good with the information or not. For me, it is important to understand why I was not able to align myself with a specific message or situation. This is another way that I have evolved personally, by trying to understand why some messages do not align with me.

Understanding myself helps me to be more centered and grounded, and this allows me to release or turn off any thought that may just be creating drama and wasting energy. Drama does not allow you to reach a resolution, due to the fact that it is an unresolved issue in your brain.

Understanding and knowing how your brain works, is crucial for a speedy healing treatment. Being able to know that you can control your thoughts and determine where you are going to invest your energy is key. Thought control allows you to release something that is not wanted such as drama, illness, sorrows or, as I call it, 'Wasted Energy Garbage.'

When we talk about control, it is important not to let past experiences or lived memories interfere with your future plans. You cannot allow your past to control your present. We do learn from previous experiences, but we should be able to let go of the situation and only keep what we have learned. The power is in today, for you to evolve, not in the past. There is no need to repeat the past over and over.

THE TIME IS NOW! It is time to begin with what you need and want in your life today! As I have been saying, throughout the book, if you create intentions and desires with consciousness, you will see results. Keep reminding yourself why you are doing all of this. You should keep these thoughts in your mind when you feel resistance that is impairing your ability to feel free while integrating new information.

Integration is a very important part of the Plant Spirit Medicine ceremony. In my experience, integration begins at the end of the 10 or 12 hour ceremony, when all participants share some of their experiences. It's the time to share or clarify any questions or concerns you may have had while on the medicine. It is important to participate and listen, as well as give your opinion. This is the beginning of the treatment that you are looking for. For me, it is the beginning of the outcome of the treatment.

I have seen people affected by the medicine to the point that they were not able to participate in the last step of the ceremony consciously. This process of integration and assimilation can continue for weeks or even months while they incorporate their discoveries and messages from the medicine.

Allow yourself to have a full experience. Don't rush to conclusions and assumptions. Just take the time to process what you just experienced during the ceremony. Understanding the importance of allowing the process to go through yourself, your body, your mind and your soul without pushing your wants is very important.

Another part of learning is to listen and be patient, while opening yourself up to the 'art of allowing.' Try to integrate these experiences organically and naturally into your lifestyle.

It is important to believe in the medicine and be open-minded. You want to be open and learn what was being presented to you by the medicine.

You should confront any fear or shadow that you may encounter during the ceremony and/or during the integration and assimilation period. You will still be under the effect of the medicine during this last step of the ceremony. Allow yourself to express your feelings and your messages. These feelings and messages will have a double purpose. They will flow through your body as you share them with the group. While you share these messages, there will be other participants who will benefit from your healing process and delivery. Understanding and wanting to work on some issues is up to you and cannot be forced. Your mind will find ways to mislead you if it has trouble with the emotions and behaviors. You must be ready, and prepared, and willing to want to change your situation and take control of your thoughts.

The integration will allow you to release any type of preconception or expectation that you may have had at the ceremony. Just take the facts that you were able to gather and work on them. Now is the time to organize and recreate yourself because the medicine allowed you to see things from a different perspective. Now, you can understand things that you were not able to before. The medicine has allowed you to learn much more about yourself. The medicine has also put you in touch with the environment, guides and ancestors, so you can comprehend things naturally from your past to your present.

This new way of seeing the issue or behavior that you originally wanted to work on should become part of your evolution, when you feel it's right and aligned with yourself after assimilation.

The change will make you a different person than you were before. These new teachings will allow you to heal or find solutions to your problems, but most important, it will allow you to evolve. You will be able to acquire these teachings and hopefully, you won't make the same mistakes again. At the very least, you will understand the consequences of such behavior. You will have the information to tackle the issue again, if you have to, and it will be ok if that happens.

It is up to the person to want to heal, learn, listen and evolve.
It is up to the person to ask for help and take charge of the issue.
It is up to the person to want to feel good.

RITUALS
There are procedures that I follow after the ceremony, and many of these steps could be considered rituals.

I have been told many times in my life that I have been a witch in past lives, so rituals are kind of 'my thing.'

It is advised not to drive after you have been under the effect of the Plant Spirit Medicine as it can alter your senses. I usually have a friend pick me up after the ceremony. I do not stay at the ceremony place and sleep, as some do. I like to come home to my own environment where I can feel free to go through the effects of the medicine.

I will not talk about the ceremony or my experiences or messages received. I will usually keep silent, and the person that picks me up will know that in advance. I prepare that person so I don't have any pressure on me, nor will I have any interference with my thoughts or messages received. For me, it is important not to have any interruption of the treatment or healing process. I take it seriously, so this is how I like to do it. This behavior is so I can continue the process of assimilation and integration of the experience.

As soon as I arrive at home, I go to the garage where I have my laundry area. If you do not have a laundry area, just undress at the entrance to your home and put your clothes in a plastic black bag to be taken to the washing machine to be washed as soon as possible. As soon as I remove my clothing, I light a sage stick and sage the clothing I was wearing at the ceremony. After I sage all of the items, I will proceed to put them in the washer, including my shoes. I wear cloth type shoes to the ceremony.

I do this to make sure that I am leaving all low energies or any energies that I should not have around me, outside my home. You need to protect your home. It is your temple. It is important, especially when you are taking time to assimilate something that is so profound from your healing treatment. It is vital that you are in a clean and open environment, free of bad energies that can really interfere with the reception of your messages. You need to be in a space that will induce you to be open, surrendering, and allow the new information to be absorbed as organically as possible.

After doing these steps upon arrival, I will remain nude and proceed, to sage myself. After the sage process, I will take a shower with Himalayan salt, pink salt or Ruda soap. I will use any cleansing herb that I feel attracted to at that time. As part of my showering experience, I receive a lot of messages, and I will allow them to flow through me. The water will be part of my cleansing and message integration. The water also helps me to relax and stimulate my crown chakra for a better flowing and better integration as the water covers my body.

I will then dry myself off and go to my bed to continue the integration process. Many times, I will not be able to sleep right away after a ceremony. Sometimes I find that I don't fall asleep until the sun comes up the next day. The important thing is for you to surrender and allow the messages and information that you are receiving, to flow as part of the integration.

Once you are able to sleep, you will continue receiving messages that are related to your broad or defined intention.

When I get up the following day, I am usually not hungry at all. I drink water, for sure, but not coffee. The water helps me to come down and ground myself. I find noises, music, TV or radio annoying and a disturbance to my thoughts. I allow myself to spend the whole day by myself writing messages and meditating, while I continue to try to understand the information that I have received in the last 24 hours. These are very important moments of the treatment for me.

As a rational and thinking person, the process of understanding and assimilating messages and information is fascinating to me. Spending a whole day in silence and allowing the after effects of the medicine to flow through my being is very pleasurable and enlightening. During this time, I recharge myself. I become emotional at times as I begin to understand the messages. For me, it is a beautiful process.

By nighttime of the day after the ceremony, I will have a light meal and go to sleep when I feel the need to, regardless of the time. I dedicate the whole day and possibly the next day, as well, to surrender as part of my healing plan.

Remember, we are all different, and we have time frames that are specific to us. Some of us will need more time to process thoughts and messages than others. So, do not rush or avoid steps, because I have news....you can't achieve that! Everything will take its course in the time needed. It usually takes me 36 hours to fully ground myself 100%. For me, that will be the second phase or step of the integration and assimilation process, with phase one being the end of the ceremony.

There is a third phase for me that I experience after the 36 hours. By the third day, I am fully grounded and back to where I used to be. Now, everything will begin to make sense. You will be able to start connecting thoughts, events, ideas and so many other things. Be open and allow the medicine to continue its work and treatment.

You will feel different now because you had the medicine. You are a new person in many ways. Now, you possess valuable information, and it is up to you how you will implement it and use it to your advantage.

The third level I mentioned can last for several days, weeks or months. You are fully conscious and you are consciously implementing your new information, and this will take time and work: spiritually, mentally and physically.
You should develop a routine to continue this process utilizing meditation, affirmations, changes in routines, and integration of new behaviors. You are in control of your own treatment and

healing and I believe you can do it!

LEARNINGS

Learnings are part of involvement. I always say that we are all capable of learning, if we want to, and are willing to put the energy into it. This is a subject that I personally believe in, and I am living proof of it.

As a typical educator, I need to define the true meaning of learning. "Learning is the relatively permanent change in a person's knowledge or behavior due to experience." We define learning as the transformative process of taking in information that, when internalized and mixed with what we already know and have experienced, changes what we know and builds on what we do.

What is learning and how do we learn? We can determine that learning occurs when we are able to gain a mental or physical grasp on a subject. The good part of this process is that we will use our newly acquired ability or knowledge in conjunction with skills and understanding that we already possess. This way, we will continue our journey of constant evolvement.

Understanding the basis of learning can assist you in having a more organic and holistic lifestyle. Allowing yourself to experience new events without putting up resistance is the key. Just let it flow and let it be.

There are three basic types of learning styles; visual, auditory and kinesthetic. To learn, we depend on our senses to process the information around us. Most people tend to use one of their senses more than the others. Open your gifts, honor them, discover them, practice them and exercise them. Take the time and energy to discover who you are and what you are about!

You need to have the desire to learn, as well as want it and feel good about it in the process. These processes cannot be imposed by anyone. For example, only you can take control of how, when, and why you will select a treatment. For a treatment or a healing process to work, you must believe in it, and you must be open to the teachings so that you can incorporate it into your routine.

Plant Spirit Medicine is a wonderful, healing medicine, and as you have heard me say,

'Once you meet the spirit of the plant, your life will never be the same.'

For me, it is a wonderful medicine that helps me reconnect, heal and evolve in a very organic and holistic manner, while I continue learning about myself.

As a rational, traditional healthcare professional, the integration of traditional psychological therapy really helped me tremendously. I am so amazed at the results. I can only say that this works very well for me. You have to discover what works best for you. Again, working with the Plant Spirit Medicine will only improve, if you do it correctly and consciously and with previous preparation.

If you would like to implement traditional psychological therapy in conjunction with the Plant Spirit Medicine, I would recommend you find a therapist who will understand alternative practices and methodologies.

I decided to combine both therapies while honoring the path I am living. I have begun to value my many years of experiences and practices in fields both professional and personal. My goal was to integrate them all as part of my treatment and behavioral changes.

I was willing to open myself up and let go of bad behaviors and patterns that were not working for me. You start to realize this after making the same mistakes many times, so, listen, study, discover yourself and learn from it. Learn what works for you. Put yourself first and go for it because you are the only one who knows exactly what you want to change and what has worked or not worked on your current journey.

The assistance of professionals is important, and I would suggest you consult a professional for advice always.

I can assure you that dedicating your time to a specific goal, in a conscious state, will lead you to success. This is based on my personal experience in manifesting my desires and intentions, not only in my professional career, but as a serial entrepreneur.

I never thought to become a serial entrepreneur, but through the years, I developed and created many successful businesses, and also became a consultant for other people's businesses.

Success will surely take you through ups and downs. You will always be learning, growing and evolving. I will just remind you to allow yourself the time to flow while you continue your evolving path.

We all evolve in different time frames, and sometimes we must go through similar messages over and over until we are evolved to the point where we fully understand the messages we are receiving.

I have been dedicating my time to continue learning about myself, my mission and my vibration. As I have been learning, and this book is proof, I am able to become a messenger of my own experiences within my journey. I hope that this sharing of messages and learnings will inspire others to discover themselves along their path.

Be safe always, and remember, when we are learning, we are honoring ourselves and our ancestors with love.

OUTCOMES

Outcomes are the results that we are looking for. They can be fantastic and wonderful or not. They come in many shapes and forms, but they can take their 'sweet time' after the implementation process.

In a more formal way, we say that outcomes are specific, measurable statements that let you know when you have reached your goals. Outcome statements describe specific changes in your knowledge, attitudes, skills and behaviors that you expected to occur as a result of your actions.

You will see results in different stages of your healing process while you are reaching for your desired goal. Don't go crazy trying to get results by following a calendar or watching a clock. Everything happens in a divined plan and time. It is important for you to support your original intention and continue to allow your process to move forward. A healing process can take longer than you want it to, but you must continue to allow it with the sole intention of feeling good while you are evolving from your current state.

There will be times when you can see results immediately. Sometimes, you will receive a message that you will be able to interpret right away, and it will allow you a very simple process of implementation. There will also be times when you will be receiving messages, and they will take much longer to assimilate. The reason this can happen is you may need to experience other events before you can assimilate this particular message. Consider it like it is: a missing link to the main message.

This is why it is so important to have a very defined and focused intention. This way, you will be able to work on that intention, looking for that specific answer. By doing this, you will allow yourself to receive other messages more naturally and without resistance, since you have already prepared yourself.

While you are working on your original intention, you may receive other healing treatments through the medicine that may be related to or supportive of your original intention. This is why you need a conscious intention prior to attending the ceremony. This will also help you to go through the assimilation and integration process while allowing you to see unexpected messages that will make sense to you when you are not so strongly under the effect of the medicine. This experience will help you understand the true and whole message that the medicine has for you while surrendering, allowing and consciously following your instincts and gifts. Embrace the experience.

JOURNAL, DIARY AND MESSAGES

Somehow, my guides and angels are whispering to me and advising me to use my educational experience to communicate some messages to you. I realize that some chapters of this book have sections with academic information, and the purpose is to generate a base line or common ground for everyone to understand. It is important for me to share, as well, that we cannot be 100% connected to Source and vibrating at a high frequency without grounding ourselves at times. The idea of being connected to Source at a high level of frequency would be totally unbalanced and unrealistic. Being able to sustain balance and patience all the time is the hardest and most valuable event in our journey.

Just think of how important it is to be connected with Earth. Being grounded is the basis of being here. It's like the base of a tree connected to the Earth and having roots and continuing to grow, while connecting with the universe.

Being able to create a journal or diary will assist you in being grounded, while gathering important information that will be useful in clarifying various messages. Keep in mind that this journal will be helpful throughout your journey.

A journal is a collection of articles, (like having your own magazine), that will be reviewed and read regularly throughout the year. A journal presents the most recent research written by experts. What this means is you will be writing great messages from experts like archangels, guides and Source. If you are receiving these messages, it means that you are ready to understand and use them; otherwise, they would not be given to you. Some messages are visual, and if you are not ready to see them, they will not be shown to you. There are messages all around us. We just need to take the time to observe them and be open to them.

Let's understand the difference between a diary and a journal. A diary is a book to record events as they happen. A journal is a book used to explore ideas that take shape. You will select which of these two styles resonates with you. I believe we always end up with a magical combination of both writing skills for a common intention and goal, but, don't be surprised if you get messages in a specific style...just go with it.

When starting a journal, look for the best space to write. Make sure that you assign a notebook specifically to this or buy a physical journal. Close your eyes and feel the message, vibrate with the message, then dive in and start writing.

When going to a ceremony, it is advisable for you to bring a notepad, or a recording device that you feel comfortable using. Make sure that you are permitted to bring these items before you go. While you are under the effect of the medicine, you will experience messages coming to you and you may want to write them down. This is not my way of doing it, but, it's up to each individual. I have seen people get a whole story as a message, and I am sure that must be fantastic, but my personal experience on transmitting or writing messages usually happens after I process the message analytically and rationally.

At times, you may experience images or visualizations that are part of your messages. It is important to keep a journal or a notepad near, so you can write down what is flowing through you.

Keep in mind that these messages or information not only happen during the time you are on the medicine, but, as I mentioned before, they will occur after, as well.

Remember that the medicine will take you to places that you need to go. The medicine will take you to areas that you need to work on, perhaps areas that you have been ignoring. Be open, be receptive and surrender to the learning experience.

I find it helpful to keep a notepad on my nightstand and one with me during the day as well. Be aware that you can also receive messages through your dreams. Be sure to write messages down as soon as you receive them. If you don't, there is a possibility that you will not remember them and will lose them. In the details of dreams is where you are going to find the most important information.

So, when you go to a Plant Spirit ceremony and take the medicine, you may be able to understand those messages immediately or in the near future. Sometimes, I get the messages fast, and other times, I am not able to receive it at its delivery time. This is why I keep reinforcing that we should not have expectations....just flow and surrender to the information.

Another reason why you should keep a journal is if you are practicing any other type of alternative medicine techniques, you can see how they relate to each other.

Take this seriously, and what may not make sense today will make total sense in a few weeks or months. If you got a message and you were able to receive it, believe me, it was for you. You just need to take the time to interpret it organically.....and you will.

Review your journey and try to connect the dots, so you can start implementing the true message in a very organic and holistic way. Believe in yourself and that everything happens for a reason. Sending love to you.

INTEGRATION OF MESSAGES

Integration of messages can come to us in many ways and forms. I believe that certain messages reappear in different ways throughout our journey, until we are ready to see them, understand them, and finally interpret them. Sometimes, we receive a message that we believe we understand, but later we see that it was not what we thought, but something totally different.

If you remember, in a previous chapter, I described my experience with the death of my partner's mom, the death his dog, and the end of our relationship. Because of those experiences, I believed that I needed to learn about the sense of loss and be more spiritual in learning about transitions. It was an obvious analogy based on events, but there was another message within this message. Throughout the implementation process of that original message, a true, deeper message was hidden.

It was hidden because I didn't know how to stay open and let the messages flow. I was getting to the conclusion prematurely, without looking at the whole picture.

We need to prepare for the messages so that when we get them, we can try to interpret and integrate them without rushing to judgment. We need to set our ego aside along with the urgency to cure our problem and concentrate consciously on connecting to our guides for confirmation.

The message for me to learn was about LETTING GO! Letting go of what I had and now no longer have such as:
- Letting go of my relationship
- Letting go of a physical body during transition

- Letting go of the emotional drama that I created in my mind

- Letting go of the apartment I shared with my partner

- Letting go of someone I thought I would spend the rest of my life with

- Letting go of fantasies

Many messages were involved with this process and many lessons are continuing to unfold even to today.

It is important to know who you are and to believe in yourself. Honor yourself and be open to these experiences even when they are painful. You can cry, scream, and feel the pain, but know that you won't stay in it. We will feel pain and let it go. It is important to know and acknowledge your fears and feelings. Be open to allow the implementation process and the time it needs to receive true messages.

I say to you, my readers, to dedicate your time, energy and gifts to the process, while believing in what you are doing. I will continue to mention the importance of consciousness with our intentions and our actions. As the universe has observation and intelligence fields, so do we, and we should use them consciously to develop our state of happiness.

Allow and surrender to this beautiful process without expectations and with an open heart. Remember that you are taking this medicine because you choose to do so. You believe in this medicine and you are ready to receive these messages because you took the time to prepare yourself for the ceremony.

You are Light!

You are Special!

You are Beautiful!

You deserve to be Happy!

CHAPTER 12: MY JOURNEY, OUTCOME & LEARNINGS

We are always evolving....
Don't expect me to be the same person I was yesterday....
I evolved, I learned and I moved on.....HF

NEW ROUTINE.... NEW ME

When you begin thinking about how to incorporate new behaviors or systems into your daily routine, it can become very overwhelming. You are talking about changing behaviors in order to help support or assist in a healing process. This component of the healing process is as important as the medicine itself, since they will work together and assist you to work in an organized and holistic process to achieve your result.

The success of this new routine will occur only if you do it consciously and responsibly, and if you are truly honoring your desire aligned with a conscious intention.

During a Plant Spirit Medicine ceremony, while I was under

the effect of the medicine, things seemed to be much simpler to me. Obviously, it was, since my conscious and subconscious were almost together, and they were allowing themselves to communicate in a very organic manner, with no barriers or ego present, as a judge of what was right or wrong. The effect of the medicine, in my case, allowed me to see things in a very clear and organic manner.

The most important thing for me to do in this chapter is to bring back that beautiful information received at the ceremony and be able to incorporate, integrate and assimilate it into my daily life routine, and hope it works for you as well.

Sometimes we can consciously understand what needs to be done, but the implementation of new ideas, routines or systems on a daily basis can be challenging. The challenge begins when trying to connect conscious thoughts with our mind, emotions, desires and goals. That is a lot, isn't it?

Think of it as if they need to all coexist together without arguing, while respecting each other's positions. Every sense has its own role and mission and, of course, negotiations and resistance will occur, among these feelings. However, no arguments or getting upset should be allowed. You need to be in control, and you need to be clear about what you want, possibly a referee, so be easy on yourself. Everything has to work together, and like on any team, there is going to be periods of learning, adjusting and communicating as part of the team effort and team work.

Be able to achieve these new changes holistically. It will only be possible if you are determined to follow your desires and you commit to doing it consciously, while honoring yourself, your peace and your balance. I'd like to clarify that I have never said that work on your part was not going to be required.

Many times, I questioned myself about the amount of work and energy that is involved in this process. Even some of my clients asked me if it was truly needed. I realized the amount of energy, dedication and work that had to be involved in trying to heal, resolve, incorporate and assimilate new behavior. Remember, the most important point is the outcome of feeling good, light and satisfied while we let go of what is not wanted. Trust me, it is so worth it and I would do everything all over again, and again.

I constantly remind myself that I have to work on things and situations as part of my evolvement in learning, personal growth, and happiness. Otherwise, everything would be to our satisfaction, and no evolution would be necessary.

The beauty of this process occurs when we see ourselves in a humble and honest mode. It is then when we begin accepting ourselves in totality with our gifts and our faults, our fears and our shadows and all areas that needs improvement.

Self-discovering is not always fun, as I mentioned in another chapter of this book. However, being in touch with your inner self is needed and important. The need to go deep and do an inner search to find the true answers is what is important in order to change.

It is essential to be 100% committed to our desires and intentions. Commitment is the first step that we need to take to be able to do this process of changing. With commitment, also comes responsibility.

Taking responsibility and being committed to wanting to be happy, wanting to feel good, being in balance and focused in your desires, is important and needed. You will begin by aligning your desires with your intentions with many other elements.

You will understand how everything needs to be aligned and vibrating in the same or similar frequency to work organically. Being able to understand these steps will help you grasp the importance and the power of your thoughts. These thoughts must be aligned with yourself, your desires, and with Source.

Your thoughts carry vibrational power, and they are as powerful as your intention. Now you can understand, by controlling your thoughts, you will be able to control the process, or at least, support the process.

It is not hard for an analytical person to rationally understand these steps. Once its importance is understood, which is the hardest part for most of us, it can be put into emotional practice. The practice will be like an agreement of these steps with your emotions, thoughts, vibrations and all of the above. It's about reaching that coexistence in a harmonious vibration, while you support and maintain these new changes needed in your routine.

When I started understanding these steps, I began to find ways to implement them in my daily routine. As part of my implementation, I went to my creative side and found ways that would assist me in holding these changes in place.

I began thinking about how I could incorporate these new changes and behaviors into my new lifestyle. I know myself, and for me personally, it has to make sense rationally first, so I began creating very little changes in my routine while working toward the goal.

It is very hard for me to maintain or sustain a new routine if the changes are very different from my current daily routine. The idea is to add and subtract a little at a time into your current routine, and not to create a whole new routine. I think that it's hard or challenging for most of us. It takes an average of 21 days to change or break a behavior with constant responsibility, work, and energy to obtain your goal.

So how do we alter or modify a current routine with new behaviors? As I mentioned before, I found success in the incorporation of little changes to my daily routine. These small changes have to make sense to YOU! In my case, it had to make sense rationally and emotionally, so it wouldn't be a surprise for my brain or my body which would be craving my old patterns.

Many times, you start changing something in your routine because you were told to by a friend or colleague. In truth, you may be receiving great advice from these individuals, but you are not that person. We are all different, and what works for them may not work for you, just for the simple reason that you cannot resonate with the suggestion or the implementation of such.

You need to know yourself so you can create and suggest new changes in your routine, so it will feel organic and natural. The idea is to begin integrating these changes into your current routine almost as if you are not even feeling it or noticing it.

Making changes in an organic mode is the easiest way to be able to sustain and maintain that new change because you will not feel the new change as something totally out of your normal behavior pattern.

For many years, I made a very common mistake. Every time I wanted to tackle a new issue in my daily routine or wanted to change a pattern or a behavior, I used to begin with a clean slate. I was able to do that so well rationally, but when the time of implementation came, it was very stressful and difficult. The implementation process was very challenging for me. Usually you will need to modify or add or subtract as I mentioned before. You will need to look at the whole picture.

When I used to start from scratch, I was not taking into consideration my current routine. I was not considering what I HAD, what I WORKED ON already, what I KNEW, what I ACHIEVED, what I FELT and ENJOYED while creating that routine. In a way, I was not honoring my work and not taking the time to take the good out of that routine and set my ego aside and admit that not EVERYTHING was not working, and allow myself to add or subtract what was not working for me NOW.

It was obvious that at one point, the routine worked, but like everything else, we evolve, and situations evolve as well, and our routine may become obsolete and need work or some type of tune up to continue contributing to our happiness.

But wait! Did I say our happiness needs to be part of the plan? Of course! For something to be sustainable in your life, it has to have some type of pleasurable feeling. That feel-good sensation must be part of the plan. That way it will be easier to make the changes. Happiness will give us the balance of the new change with the resistance and ego. We just need to concentrate on feeling good, and that will be another motivator to do it.

So, I started understanding that I was not taking into consideration, my likes and dislikes, so frustration and ego began to be more pronounced in the process. Being able to avoid reaching this level of frustration or confusion is the beginning of success. However, most of us, when we feel frustrated and confused, tend to just drop a project. The reason for that is, it just doesn't give us any type of pleasure, so, remember pleasure must be part of your plan.

The success for me was based on being able to implement a new idea without discarding what was already learned and proven to work. The key is being able to incorporate changes that will improve the current plan in a non-threatening manner to your body, mind and spirit.

The first step is to determine what the ultimate goal is to achieve and write down how you   feel organically about the changes. While you do your inner search, listen to your inner voice and think about the changes that must happen to begin your process for healing, or for any other goal. I believe that this process can be applied to any type of routine.

For example, I suffer from Acid Reflux for which I've been taking medication for many years. I wanted to stop taking medication because I wanted to have a more natural and artificial medication-free lifestyle. This was a great moment and opportunity to see how I could use Complementary and Alternative methods in my own lifestyle, as well.

This is one of the messages that I've been receiving since I began my first class on Energy Healing studies. I knew that I was entering into this new field with the intention of personal growth and healing, and also as a person of service. I knew somehow that I needed to do this study so I could work on the current clinical path that I've been on for over 25 years. and connect them somehow. This was very clear, and my intention was set from the very beginning. You will see by the time that you finish reading this chapter, how important it is to listen to your intuition, guides and messages, while following your intention and desires.

One of the messages that I also received during my participation in the Plant Spirit Medicine ceremony was the guides showing me how to resolve my issues. They showed me how to take back the control of situations, in general. They showed me how I had been doing it for others, but that it was time now for me to do it for myself.

The medicine will always help you in a mysterious and intelligent way. It will holistically lead you to the areas that you need to work on. This is why it is so important to be open and willing to receive the messages without resistance and expectations. Believe it or not, it is part of the treatment that you need.

These messages and treatments that you will receive during the ceremony are very important for you to pay attention to, and you should write them down to remember later on. In my case, my mind and thought process takes at least 24 hours to properly process them. Usually, I will get the messages the following day, and sometimes, I will get the message in its totality with sub-messages and interpretation even up to a week after the day of the ceremony.

This book is an example of how the messages received during and after the ceremony are still amplifying and detailing themselves while I am writing them in this book. I believe that communication and messaging is my mission, and this book is the confirmation. While I keep receiving messages and details on them, I will be just a channel for them and a person of service.

I hope that this explanation on the steps that I took as part of my plan can benefit you or shed some light on your new routine approach.

Once I set that clear desire and I decided to take responsibility to support that desire, I began to think about how I could achieve my intention and desire with some manifestation.

WOW... now we are talking about manifestation!... a great moment and our ultimate goal in this case. (I was called a MANIFESTOR once and I still laugh about it...but am I?... Can you be?)

Therefore, when I had the desire to stop taking the acid reflux medication, I questioned myself, "Why do I want to do it? What would be the benefits? How committed am I to finding a way to stop taking the medication? Am I committed to this change?

Am I willing to concentrate and invest time and energy into it?"

Let me mention that my acid reflux is not the most common type that will manifest in stomach pains or burn symptoms. My condition is called Laryngopharyngeal Reflux, LPR. Laryngopharyngeal Reflux is a condition in which acid that is made in the stomach travels up the esophagus and gets into the throat. Symptoms include sore throat and an irritated larynx (voice box), and treatments consist mostly of lifestyle changes.

As a professional singer, I was preparing myself for a show and I realized that I was not able to have perfect pitch on some notes. I was feeling as if I had a cold in my throat, but no other symptoms were present, and this condition was interfering with my singing.

If we want to go deeper into this situation, it was affecting my Chakra #5, the Chakra of communication. I will not expand on this subject as it is too extensive and passionate to talk about very lightly. I will surely be talking about chakras and their importance in another book very soon.

At the beginning, I listened to my mother and friend telling me that it was nothing. My mom, a nurse, was visiting me with my father, and she told me that it was all in my mind. She meant well, since she knew that I did not have any fever or any other symptoms and I was feeling fine. She did tell me to go to a specialist, but not to worry about it. My friends were telling me that it was just a cold... Nobody knew about my condition but everyone was trying to help me with their recommendations. This is an example of how important it is to know yourself and listen to your inner voice and intuition.

I decided to go to a specialist and begin the clinical search of the investigation. I went to five different doctors who specialized in ear, nose and throat, otolaryngologists, because I was not satisfied with the results that I was getting. I was so focused in my mind and so sure that I had something else or something related to another illness. I didn't want to be ill, but I was not able to understand how I could have Acid Reflux without pain or symptoms. The funny part is, as I am writing this, at this precise moment, a message came to me, saying...

YOU WERE NOT PAYING ATTENTION!
There WERE symptoms, and you just didn't pay attention to them. "Thank you, Angels for the message, and you are correct; I was not listening, for sure."

After visiting so many specialists and gathering their reports, to my surprise, they all came to the same conclusion. My last doctor, (Doctor #5) said to me, "Listen, I am not sure why you do not want to see this for what it is, and I suggest you stop looking any further."

Mind you that I had over 100 needles stuck into me to check for allergies, among other investigations on this issue. I realized that I needed to accept and embrace it and take responsibility for my current situation.

I wonder why I put up so much resistance at that time. The truth is that I needed to let go of the control. The message for me was to let go of the telenovela drama that I had in my mind, telling me that I had something else. It is important to see how an instinct can become an obsession that will not contribute anything positive to your journey. This mental garbage is just an interruption. As you can see, the drama did not help me, and I could have stopped it if I had been more grounded and was paying better attention. I knew that I needed to let go of the control, so I surrendered and accepted the diagnosis and started to make some changes to better my current situation.

I looked into how to stop taking acid reflux medication and

found that it could be resolved with a change of diet, reduction of stress and weight loss.

I knew that a change of diet could be modified very easily, but as an 82% Italian descendent from Argentina, it was going to be challenging. I knew that most of the food related to my culture would always involve some vegetables that I was not supposed to be eating with acid reflux.

My challenge was on! And I questioned myself, "How can I eat meals without tomatoes, onions, or even drink wine or any other type of alcohol?" (I'm laughing while I am writing and I can feel Mr. Ego challenging me).

My first challenge was to take responsibility for the things that I was willing to change and could change, and those things that I was not willing to change, or knew would be too hard to leave out of my diet.

I believe that, in any event that will change your lifestyle, you may have some compromises to make. I believe that part of the commitment and success in any plan is the ability to be flexible while taking on responsibility for the decisions you make. Rigid things are not flexible. If you enter into a rigid diet or treatment without any type of compromise or flexibility, it will not work for you. I knew it would not work for me. I knew that I needed to be creative. Creativity could become your best friend, as part of the art of implementation of a plan, while respecting your needs, wants and desires.

I then made a list of things that I was willing to change and a list of things that I was not willing to change. Sometimes the things that I was not willing to change are the ones that I know will create some type of conflict with some area of my persona, but the idea was to make the changes the easiest and friendliest to my daily routine, in order to help me achieve my goal.

This will help you create a more doable and realistic new routine for yourself. Remember you want to alter your current routine. You want to implement new behaviors or new things into your current routine. While making these changes, you will not feel threatened or challenged to sustain the adjustment to the current routine in your life. You want to add new behaviors, so you can start seeing results. At the end of the day, you need to be happy with the routines that you are changing. If you can celebrate and support the new, small changes with a clear desire responsibly, big changes will support themselves since it's not going to be a challenge or an unpleasant change in your daily routine.

Therefore, at that time I was able to commit myself to a change. I felt good. I felt good because I was committed to achieve and manifest a desire, so, I began thinking about my daily routine. Knowing myself, I knew that I could change my diet and decrease the amount of food that was not appropriate for my symptoms. I took responsibility to stop eating greasy food and reduce the number of tomatoes and onions I ate. I also knew that exercise was a very important step. I knew that I needed to lose weight as part of the supportive plan, but it was not my primary goal or intention.

That is another challenge by itself! Isn't it? Nevertheless, I did not put all my intention into losing weight. I refocused and I went back to my initial desire, which was stopping medication for my acid reflux and resolving, my singing issue due to the inflammation that I was experiencing in my larynx.

I was very happy to see how everything was aligning organically with my new adjustment in my lifestyle. I did lose some weight, and that helped to support my goal. I will accept this weight loss due to the changes in my diet as an incentive. This is another way to support and sustain the new changes in one's lifestyle.

Do you see how everything is integrated? At this time, I was able to understand how changing my diet, along with the commitment that I was making to myself, would not only reduce or eliminate the medication, but also help me achieve other goals. It was important to see that taking control was what I was learning, taking control and wanting to resolve an issue, taking control of my happiness and feeling good.

This is when you need to remind yourself to stop the drama, take charge, be responsible and make the changes needed for you to feel good and help you vibrate to your highest level.

This is a simple way to make yourself happy, once you are committed and ready to confront your fears and challenges.

At this time, I also began researching other ways to support and assist myself with this new change in my lifestyle. I was drinking a lot of water as part of my daily routine, and in my research, I was able to find information on alkaline water and its positive effect on acid reflux.

As part of my daily routine, I was always pushing myself to drink more water. I was drinking filtered tap water and bottled water. I was proud of myself that I was into that routine of hydrating myself and flushing my system to keep it healthy and running. Now, alkaline water has become part of my daily routine.

Also, my routine was complemented with a vitamin regimen as well. I learned a lot about herbs and their effect in the body. Being healthy and eating healthy was becoming my priority with all these changes.

I want to mention that this process took me several years to get to where I am today. One of the reasons was that I did not have the information that I currently possess. The beauty of this process is that once you place a conscious intention into your hands, that intention will be with you always. The routine can always be altered, and adjusted because you are consciously and continually doing what is needed for you to feel good. Remember that God, Source, and/or the Universe will give you the results that you need and deserve, so, here is another confirmation for the power of a clear and conscious intention.

After my research on alkaline water, I began drinking it as part of my daily routine. This was a very effortless change for me. This is a confirmation on how you need to implement new things, behaviors and systems into your life without completely erasing your current routine. After I began implementing the alkaline water, I was able to find other resources with the same purpose of controlling my LPR.

Covid-19, in a way assisted me to connect a few things in my routine. I began searching how to improve my immune system to protect myself from the virus, besides just washing my hands and covering my face, as well as social distancing. During this scary and uncertain virus time, I began concentrating on natural herbs and vitamins to boost my immune system. When I was putting my supportive vitamin regimen together, I came across a new discovery for myself.

I have been taking probiotics for a while, and I believe in their benefit. During my research, I've learned the effect and benefit of Lactobacillus Acidophilus, as a probiotic for acid reflux. Lactobacillus acidophilus is a type of bacteria found in one's intestines. Probiotic supplements containing Lactobacillus acidophilus are commonly used for heartburn and reflux symptoms. Probiotics or "friendly" bacteria may help maintain a balance in the digestive system between good and harmful bacteria.

The idea of taking a specific type of probiotic, that could also help me with the acid reflux problem, was heaven to my ears. I began implementing the new idea. I supplemented the current probiotic that I was currently taking with Lactobacillus Acidophilus, so this way, I was fine tuning my plan and routine without losing my intention.

As someone with a clinical mind and creativity, I put two and two together. I started taking the alkaline water with this new probiotic. I began combining both of them in my daily routine. Instead of taking my acid reflex medication, I was able to supplement it with a glass of alkaline water and one pill from this probiotic. I was able to feel the difference within a week. This will also prove that my daily routine was minimally altered with very little effort. It did not require much on my part to change my daily routine, and it was easy to keep it up and maintain it.

For me, it was important to be happy. Being happy, while doing good things for our bodies organically and holistically is my motto.

CHAPTER 13: INTEGRATION OF MESSAGES

You start being happy the day that you choose
to make yourself happy...HF

LET IT GO....LETTING GO...

Letting go is an easy thing to say but a hard thing to do, consciously, without lying or deceiving yourself. Letting go is a process that must be accomplished in a complete state of consciousness for a true healing to begin. Obviously, our emotions must be aligned with the intention, so our ego will not interfere or detain the process. Letting go is possible, but only if you really want it. It is a very challenging process, but that doesn't mean that it is too hard to do it. The most difficult part is to prepare yourself and take responsibility for your desire.

Learning this process was always presented to me by source, in many ways, throughout my life, and I'm sure it was presented to you as well. What I realized is that I was not observing, comprehending or paying attention to the messages through the events that were presented to me.

My journey to San Pedro and Ayahuasca began as part of my intention to let go of my sorrows and my aching heart.

I knew that I needed to let go of feelings, emotions and drama that were recurring in my mind. I knew that, cognitively and rationally, in order to do this, I had to set my ego aside and welcome peace and balance as a priority in my life.

While I am writing this, messages keep coming to me, and they continue to corroborate and clarify my thoughts. In passing them on to you, I want to be sure that I can be as clear as possible, for you to grasp them 'in the raw' as I receive them.

Everything started when my ex-partner's mother passed to the other side, in New York, a few months ago. She had been battling cancer for many years, but it was spreading its power throughout her body. My relationship with her was always cordial and pleasant. Her situation was expected, and she was very involved with the process, and willing to flow with her situation without resisting the transition.

I was in Florida and my ex-partner was in New York with his mom. I was waiting for the phone call to let me know it was time to go to New York. I think it's relevant here to say that he was my partner when all of this happened with his mom. He called me and said he needed me to be there, so I went. At the time, I was dealing with the Covid-19 issue in Florida and with my business.

I need to interject something here that will be relevant later. During my years of learning to be an Energy Healer, I always wanted to assist individuals with their transition to the other side. After learning and working with the angels, my desire consciously increased while working with the Archangels, on a daily basis. One of my Archangels is Azrael, and every night, I would talk to him and ask him to prepare me to be of assistance if someone needed me to help them cross over. Azrael is the angel who is responsible, in the angelic realm, to assist with the transporting of souls after death. In contrast to some negative concepts about angels of death, Azrael's role as Angel of death is a benevolent one.

I am explaining all of this because I was able to assist my partners' mother, along with the angels, Azrael, Gabriel and Michael throughout the whole process. I was not just there for her, but for the whole family and my partner as well. I didn't know them at all, but our Italian roots, united us in a land of ancestors and sounds that didn't need much introduction to feel like family. They had no idea of my intention, and I wasn't going to tell them. Some of them knew that I was an Energy Healer, and they were waiting for me to do some Reiki and some sound healing with my Tibetan singing bowls. I felt peace and love as well as a very emotional tie to this new experience and process.

One day, after finishing a Reiki session, I became very emotional when I was working on her 5th. chakra with her angels, Chamuel and Gabriel. Tears started flowing down my cheeks like two rivers. I let those tears run without wiping them and finished the session. I felt the energy flowing while she was resting, and she opened her eyes slowly every now and then. I observed her daughter in the room and her son meditating. They were benefitting from the process as well. It became a group healing. After I finished the treatment, I went immediately to the restroom to ground myself by washing my hands and my face.

While I was in the restroom, I heard someone say, "Wow, her bags are full of fluids." My partner's mom had some tubes connected to her such as catheters for urine and drainage. I didn't know that before the treatment, those bags were always empty. I knew that I was able to unblock some areas, so her energy was able to flow. In a way, she was able to let go of those fluids and release them very calmly. Letting go was my message, but I was not seeing it yet. I was more concerned about the drama and the transition and the comfort of others, and I was not paying attention to my mission of evolving or understanding my message to be learned.

My feelings about this event that I was experiencing reminded me of feelings I had in my youth about one day being able to dedicate and study that link that I thought was missing, but, was it really missing?

In the last few days of my partner's mom's transitioning, I was with her alone, holding space for her, and communicating with Azrael and Chamuel (her Archangel), while following with my hearing, the monotonous sound of the breathing machine in the room. The sound was comfortable and steady, and I was able to vibrate to that decibel frequency as I began to channel and communicate with my spiritual guides and Angels. While I was closing my eyes to communicate with the guides, I felt the need to look at her chest and I observed her breathing begin to change. Her heart was slowing down and her breathing started to become long and slow. I was able to see the clinical change in her. My intention was just to be with her for strength and support, to ease her transition without fear and help her to remain calm and comfortable.

I called the rest of the family who were in the kitchen preparing something for her to eat. I must admit that being able to be part of this specific moment was a blessing for me, personally, while being able to assist her and the family to go through this event. The angels were all around us, and the process was seamless and peaceful.

Her funeral was very conservative and complicated due to the emerging problem of Covid-19. My partner asked me to sing a contemporary version of Ave Maria, as part of his mother's service. He accompanied me on the piano while a snowstorm blew outside. Between the emotions, tears, and not being able to warm up my voice, I asked angel Gabriel to help me to perform my best for her and the family.

I realized that I needed to let go of my fears, concern and ego and continue with my true work. I had a feeling and a need to conclude my mission, as an assistant and person of service, in an organic manner.

For me, it was natural to put my emotions in song and vibrate to a higher level. It was part of my communication with God and the universe. I knew that I needed to use my music to complete the healing process. I used one of the gifts that had always accompanied me throughout my whole life, and after so many years, I realized that music was my way to practice my connection with God, the universe and my religion.

I remember sitting in the choir section of the church before I sang, asking for help with my singing. I glanced up and saw the angel Gabriel surrounded by baby angels in a celestial fresco. I felt the connection and I just stared at the image, almost mesmerized. Once again, I received the message of letting go. Who cares if your voice isn't warmed up, just be yourself, do what you have to do, send healing sounds through your voice, celebrate and honor the process. It was emotional and encouraging for me to experience those messages, and with them came peace, confirmation and love. Then I let go. I let go of the fear of not sounding my best, the fear of not hitting the high notes, and the fear of getting too emotional. All I needed to do was let go of the fears and send love to everyone.

As it turned out, I entered a state of transfixion and I was able to sing the whole song without even realizing that I was singing. I was able to vibrate in such a high frequency that I could not even remember doing it. I just remember seeing everyone with tears in their eyes as I felt a healing going through me. When I was finished singing, I was able to breathe and did not have a memory of actually singing it. It was celestial.

After I returned home to Florida, two weeks later, I experienced the death of my partner's service dog. It was very hard as it was unexpected and very sudden. Right before he transitioned, he came down the stairs, looked at me and my partner and passed in a very peaceful manner. My partner had had this dog for a very long time, and it was so hard to hear him scream and cry. It was a very powerful moment, and it touched my soul deeply.

Surely, this was going to be enough loss for a while, but I learned how to trust my instincts and my gut feelings. I knew another loss was coming. It was the loss of my relationship with my partner. We were in the process of moving into a new place for the first time. I was so shocked. I had just assisted everyone with a smooth transition and now this. I realize now that I was just feeling sorry for myself. I somehow stopped that feeling immediately, and I looked for the lesson that was going to come out of all of this loss.

I had to start thinking about what to do, and what the reasons were that so much loss of love, so much pain, and physical departures were happening around me and so close together. I knew that I needed help in order for me to continue in a stable and healthy state, so I turned to a Plant Spirit Medicine ceremony. I knew it was what I needed.

All of this was happening in the middle of the Covid-19 pandemic. Not only was I losing my relationship, dreams and plans, I was losing part of my business and trips that I was planning to Europe as well. My routine was disrupted, since I was not able to work due to the 'stay at home order.' I was not creating, producing or working during that time.

As a thinker, with a clinical mind, I had to begin psychological therapy in order to support and understand all of the changes in my life in a conscious manner. My brain needed to process these losses in a more rational way. It was important for me to combine the clinical psychological therapy with the messages that I was receiving and with the Plant Spirit Medicine. I knew that was the healing that I needed.

As I am writing this book, I am starting to realize the true messages and meanings within the original message. It was to go deeper into the true message that God wanted me to experience, see and understand.

This book is based on the messages received through the Plant Spirit Medicine ceremony, but are amplified in detail now, at this moment, as I write this to you. My learning and my experience will be a great help to others. I am hearing the voices of Raphael and Gabriel whispering in my ear, 'You needed to learn these things and to start working on them.'

I realized that the messages I was receiving before and after my treatment at the ceremony, was not just about losing a person or an emotional or material item. The message was more important and deeper than that. The message for me to learn was about 'letting go.' The death of my ex-partner's mother and the loss of the dog were to show me how one leaves the physical body behind and the soul continues its mission. We all speak of this, but to actually witness and live through it and be so immersed in it, is different and somehow, more real. The physical body is just a body, but the soul transition is part of the evolution of the soul.

The message that finally hit home for me is that we do not have people or things forever. I needed to let go, emotionally. I needed to learn, while assisting someone to cross over, that letting go of a loved one is part of the evolvement of your soul, as well as being a part of life. I was shown physically and emotionally, not only to see how this happens, but to learn from their transition and not just stay in the drama of being egotistical and mourning these physical bodies.

My relationship, which I thought was growing and on steady ground, vanished unexpectedly. I realized that I was basing all of my happiness on others and not taking care of me, and therefore, depleting myself. I had to work on that first, so I could understand the importance of that.

I can understand now that learning is not just what is visible, but what is in my thoughts and mind. I just needed to learn how to let go, period. It was revealed to me at the Plant Spirit Medicine ceremony that I needed to stop the drama, learn and let go.

As part of my daily plan for healing, I began to meditate consciously. I discovered that guided, hypnotic meditations, as well as regular meditations helped me a lot. I started doing them before I got up from the bed in the morning, and again, when I got back into bed at night. I started practicing affirmations and other methods to let the process begin, while remembering all that I was shown at the ceremony. Leaving the drama behind and letting go....

I created a positive mantra to counter my painful thoughts. I also created a physical distance from my ex-partner, so I could allow space in my heart to heal. It was also very important to control my impulses and other negative thoughts, as they would only add to the drama.

I had to remind myself to be kind to me. I tried not to question myself so much, and I allowed emotions and feelings to come for a while, but not to stay too long. This technique helped me to begin controlling my sad thoughts. At times, I did let the negative feelings flow. Did you hear the word, FLOW? Feel it and let it go!

Accept that the other person may not see the situation the way you do. Understand the other person and stop judging. Be able to put yourself first and engage in self-care as part of your daily soul caresses.

Messages do come to us all the time, every day, and it takes time to really grasp and understand them.

I still have in my mind, the minute my partner's mom crossed over and my time with her alone in that room in New York. I know that we both felt the presence of the Angel, Azrael. I can see why we were together for this lesson. We both had one to learn... letting go... and we did just that with a room full of angels, myself and ANGELa in her bed.

Before I go...

I received a message from the Angel, Raziel, to include this in my book, so others can begin discovering their own journey, and the fact that we are all transitioning. It is important to go back and see that the messages can be deeper than we originally thought. Thank you, thank you, thank you.

Every day that I worked on this book, my personal vibration began to emotionally connect with all my senses and my mind. Something very unusual happened to me. These feelings allowed me to reach a level of confidence, while a feeling of pleasure guided me while I was doing it.

A fountain of emotions, sensations and on occasion, tears flowed down my face without a specific reason. I asked myself, 'why the tears?' and then I reminded myself to just let them flow. Let those tears go. Let it go. I was connecting with the spirit of the plant's medicine, allowing me to continue seeing my issues through a magnifying lens.

The last time I attended a Plant Spirit ceremony was unique and quite different from any other time. It was my journey, but a journey to be shared with those who were intended to read my messages.

Always remember, every time you receive and share the Plant Spirit Medicine, you receive a message. That message is intended for the receiver as well as the one imparting it. We are always healing and learning, and in turn, we are also healing and teaching those around us as well.

One day, my therapist, Soledad, asked me to describe in one sentence 'what was love, acceptance and my mission.' She advised me that it could be tricky. Something inside me told me to write a sentence right after her request. I took an instant, closed my eyes and just flowed with my inner self searching for the sentence that she requested. And I wrote:

'Flow with love while we accept what we deserve with the sole purpose of our evolution in a state of peace, balance and harmony; mentally, physically, emotionally and spiritually.'

After I wrote the statement, I read it five times, and the idea of flowing was my way of letting go of the resistance and the ego that try to manage or control my feelings and thoughts.

Love. I do, or try to do everything based on love, especially when I talk about my mission. Your mission should always be based on love, love for what you believe and want to work for. Put love out into the universe for your evolution and for the evolution of others.

Your acceptance should always be with love, surrounding yourself with what it is. Accepting today and what is unfolding in a divine and planned manner. Surrender is accepting; not failing. It is the beautiful feeling of not putting up resistance to what is coming on your journey. Instead, be able to enjoy, learn and evolve on your path in life.

'What You Deserve'....What a great way of saying you should accept what is in your life now and what was in your past lives as well. You deserve the learning and the teachings, but also the recognition of what was learned in past lives also. Honoring our ancestors. Honoring today. You cannot change what has already happened, but you can modify what will happen in your future with consciousness and work, if it is part of your divined plan.

'The Soul Purpose of Evolution'.....Evolving is, and will always be my purpose, academically, spiritually and as a human being, consciously and unconsciously. Being open to the NEW and not just staying with the OLD.

'In a State of Peace, Balance and Harmony'....After a very dark moment in my life, and a deep inner search, I am not surprised that these three words come to me as they are the very definition of my happiness.

'Mentally, Physically, Emotionally and Spiritually'.....I believe in the coexistence of these four levels to make a person happy. They support each other as the greatest creation of humankind's stability and happiness. When these four levels are aligned and vibrating at their highest harmony, I believe they connect us to God, Source, the universe and pure love.

As I conclude this book of my Journey to San Pedro and Ayahuasca, I wish you happiness, love and healing energies through my written word. All healing begins with gratefulness and humbleness.

Remember, you have the control over your happiness and how you want to approach events. Prepare yourself for your journey. Learn who you truly are. Breathe love and exhale negative thoughts.

Choose happiness and love, and surrender to what it is without resistance. Surrender to who you are and let go of what is not supposed to be.

I LOVE YOU... BE SAFE! ... and Thank you, thank you, thank you.

ACKNOWLEDGEMENT

Special thanks to my friend Cindy VanDusen and Jerry Ruderman as Editors for this book and for their support throughout my journey, delivering my messages to you.

To my dear friend and colleague SoBe Cantillano for her support and love.

To LIFE...

We come to a physical body not to suffer, but to evolve, grow and be happy.

AUTHOR CONTRIBUTION

I would like to recognize Cindy VanDusen for her dedication, understanding, and support while writing this Journey to Plant Spirit Medicine.

She is a friend and contributor, not only to my life, but to this book as well.

She was able to follow me on this journey and transcribe the messages that I received from my Guides and Angels, while editing the book at the same time.

Her personal and professional skills, as well as her beautiful soul, is what makes this book flow, while being delivered to you, the readers, with love, balance, and understanding.

Cindy, from the bottom of my heart, thank you.

ABOUT THE AUTHOR

Humberto Fortuna

 Humberto Fortuna, MA, MS, was born in Buenos Aires, Argentina in 1968 where he earned his first Master of Arts degree at age 20. He came to the US in 1989 where he began his career in the Health Care field in South Florida. He specialized in Social Services for the geriatric population, concentrating in Alzheimer's and related Dementias. He received his second Master's Degree in Health Care Administration with concentration in Long Term Care from Lynn University, Florida, in 1998. He received a Post Graduate Certificate in Aging Studies in 1999. In the same year, as a Serial Entrepreneur, he created his own company; Placement Counselors Corporation. He also created Scoop for Seniors Publishing, Papinos LLC, and is publisher of 55+ Magazine, currently available in the SE region of Florida for the past 10 yrs. He currently has his own private practice as a Geriatric Specialist and won the Caregivers award for a book he co-wrote with Cindy VanDusen. He became a Certified Angel Healer Practitioner, Certified Energy Healer Practitioner, and a Certified Past Life Regressions and Akashic Records Practitioner. He also became a Certified Sound Healer and Reiki Master among other modalities. He is fusing his knowledge and experience with all these new techniques and philosophies to further his practice as an Energy Healer while dedicating his time to educating and promoting Alternative and Complementary Medicine with a Clinical Mind. Humberto is currently working on his third book "The Root

of Business Conscious Manifestation" and continues to educate
through workshops and seminars. info@humbertofortuna.com

BOOKS BY THIS AUTHOR

Everything You Need To Ask When Selecting An Assisted Living Facility

OVER 500 QUESTIONS TO ASK BE IN CHARGE OF YOUR SEARCH STEP BY STEP GUIDANCE AND ORGANIZATION The definitive, must have guide for Baby Boomers today and for their future! While helping their parents select an Assisted Living Facility today, they are educating and preparing themselves for THEIR future as well. IN ONE DAY, the reader can select an Assisted Living Facility for themselves or for their loved one by using this guide. With over 500 questions to ask, the reader will be assured that he or she is making the absolute, best decision. This guide covers subjects such as Nursing, Accommodations, Licenses, Contracts, Nutrition, Activities, Safety and more. This guide will put the reader in charge of the search so that they won't be sold something that he or she may not need or be appropriate. The authors, with their combined experience of over 42 years in the health care field, take you through the world of Assisted Living and make you feel as though you are "sitting down and chatting" with them in your living room. The goal of the authors is "to educate and therefore protect" the senior population.

REFERENCES

https://en.wikipedia.org/Mircea_Eliade

https://modernwitchdoctor.com/witchdoctor-blog/f/grow-ing-your-mesa

https://en.wikipedia.org.wiki.Witchcraft in Latin America# cite note:3-2

https://en.wikipedia.org.wiki.Witchcraft in Latin America# cite note:4-3

https://en.wikipedia.org.wiki.Icaro#cite note:Nicole-1

https://awaken.com/2020/09/the-brutal-mirror/

https://www.psychologytoday.com/us/blog/culturally-speak-ing/2019/12/introducing-ayahuasca

https://qz.com/963683/the-ayahuasca-ceremony-is-going-under-the-scientific-method-microscope/

https://www.frontiersin.org/articles/10.3389/fn-ins.2018.00563/full

https://www.mindbodygreen.com/0-14913/what-to-expect-during-an-ayahuasca-ceremony.html
https://www.pulsetours.com/the-process/

https://www.theworldisallyours.com/how-to-raise-your-vibration.html

https://www.mindbodygreen.com/0-14913/what-to-expect-during-an-ayahuasca-ceremony.html

https://awaken.com/2020/09/the-brutal-mirror/

https://www.psychologytoday.com/us/blog/culturally-speaking/2019/12/introducing-ayahuasca

https://qz.com/963683/the-ayahuasca-ceremony-is-going-under-the-scientific-method-microscope/

https://www.frontiersin.org/articles/10.3389/fnins.2018.00563/full

https://www.ncbi.nlm.nik.gov/pmc/articles/PMC6182612

https://www.verywellmind.com/how-long-does-mescaline-stay-in-your-system-80281

https://www.pharmadrugtest.com/urine-drug-tests/95-mescaline-urine-test.html

https://en.wikipedia.org/wiki/Soul_dualism

https://en.wikipedia.org/wiki/Healing

https://www.afterlife.coach.after-life-blog/2017/3/4/why -i-quit-ayahuasca-shamanism

http://entheonation.com/blog/how-to-be-an-ayahuasca-shaman/

https://www.ncbi.nlm.nik.gov/pmc/articles/PMC6182612

https://www.verywellmind.com/how-long-does-mescaline-stay-in-your-system-80281

https://www.pharmadrugtest.com/urine-drug-tests/95-mescaline-urine-test.html

https://www.ncbi.nlm.nik.gov/pmc/articles/PMC6182612/

Zeus A. Salazar (2007). "Faith healing in the Phillipines: An historical perspective" (PDF). Asian Studies. 43 (2v): 1-5

Swancutt, Katherine; Mazard, Mireille (2018). Animism beyond the Soul: Ontology, Reflexivity, and the Making of Anthropological Knowledge, New York: Berghahn Books. P. 102. ISBN 9781785338656.